OPPOSING
VIEWPOINTS®
SERIES

Interracial America

Other Books of Related Interest:

Opposing Viewpoints Series

International Adoptions

At Issue Series

Racial Profiling

Current Controversies Series

Racism

"Congress shall make no law . . . abridging the freedom of speech, or of the press."

First Amendment to the US Constitution

The basic foundation of our democracy is the First Amendment guarantee of freedom of expression. The Opposing Viewpoints series is dedicated to the concept of this basic freedom and the idea that it is more important to practice it than to enshrine it.

OPPOSING VIEWPOINTS® SERIES

Interracial America

Noah Berlatsky, Book Editor

GREENHAVEN PRESS
A part of Gale, Cengage Learning

GALE
CENGAGE Learning·

Detroit • New York • San Francisco • New Haven, Conn • Waterville, Maine • London

Elizabeth Des Chenes, *Managing Editor*

© 2012 Greenhaven Press, a part of Gale, Cengage Learning.

Gale and Greenhaven Press are registered trademarks used herein under license.

For more information, contact:
Greenhaven Press
27500 Drake Rd.
Farmington Hills, MI 48331-3535
Or you can visit our Internet site at gale.cengage.com

For product information and technology assistance, contact us at

Gale Customer Support, 1-800-877-4253
For permission to use material from this text or product, submit all requests online at www.cengage.com/permissions

Further permissions questions can be emailed to permissionrequest@cengage.com

Articles in Greenhaven Press anthologies are often edited for length to meet page requirements. In addition, original titles of these works are changed to clearly present the main thesis and to explicitly indicate the author's opinion. Every effort is made to ensure that Greenhaven Press accurately reflects the original intent of the authors. Every effort has been made to trace the owners of copyrighted material.

Cover Image copyright © David Young-Wolff/Photographer's Choice/Getty Images.

LIBRARY OF CONGRESS CATALOGING-IN-PUBLICATION DATA

Interracial America / Noah Berlatsky, book editor.
p. cm. -- (Opposing viewpoints)
Includes bibliographical references and index.
ISBN 978-0-7377-5727-9 (hardcover) -- ISBN 978-0-7377-5728-6 (pbk.)
1. United States--Race relations. 2. United States--Ethnic relations. 3. Minorities--United States. 4. United States--Social conditions. I. Berlatsky, Noah.
E184.A1I585 2011
305.800973--dc23

2011017994

Printed in the United States of America
1 2 3 4 5 6 7 15 14 13 12 11

Contents

Chapter 3: What Policies Promote Opportunities for People of All Races?

Why Consider Opposing Viewpoints?

> "The only way in which a human being can make some approach to knowing the whole of a subject is by hearing what can be said about it by persons of every variety of opinion and studying all modes in which it can be looked at by every character of mind. No wise man ever acquired his wisdom in any mode but this."
>
> *John Stuart Mill*

In our media-intensive culture it is not difficult to find differing opinions. Thousands of newspapers and magazines and dozens of radio and television talk shows resound with differing points of view. The difficulty lies in deciding which opinion to agree with and which "experts" seem the most credible. The more inundated we become with differing opinions and claims, the more essential it is to hone critical reading and thinking skills to evaluate these ideas. Opposing Viewpoints books address this problem directly by presenting stimulating debates that can be used to enhance and teach these skills. The varied opinions contained in each book examine many different aspects of a single issue. While examining these conveniently edited opposing views, readers can develop critical thinking skills such as the ability to compare and contrast authors' credibility, facts, argumentation styles, use of persuasive techniques, and other stylistic tools. In short, the Opposing Viewpoints Series is an ideal way to attain the higher-level thinking and reading skills so essential in a culture of diverse and contradictory opinions.

In addition to providing a tool for critical thinking, Opposing Viewpoints books challenge readers to question their own strongly held opinions and assumptions. Most people form their opinions on the basis of upbringing, peer pressure, and personal, cultural, or professional bias. By reading carefully balanced opposing views, readers must directly confront new ideas as well as the opinions of those with whom they disagree. This is not to simplistically argue that everyone who reads opposing views will—or should—change his or her opinion. Instead, the series enhances readers' understanding of their own views by encouraging confrontation with opposing ideas. Careful examination of others' views can lead to the readers' understanding of the logical inconsistencies in their own opinions, perspective on why they hold an opinion, and the consideration of the possibility that their opinion requires further evaluation.

Evaluating Other Opinions

To ensure that this type of examination occurs, Opposing Viewpoints books present all types of opinions. Prominent spokespeople on different sides of each issue as well as well-known professionals from many disciplines challenge the reader. An additional goal of the series is to provide a forum for other, less known, or even unpopular viewpoints. The opinion of an ordinary person who has had to make the decision to cut off life support from a terminally ill relative, for example, may be just as valuable and provide just as much insight as a medical ethicist's professional opinion. The editors have two additional purposes in including these less known views. One, the editors encourage readers to respect others' opinions—even when not enhanced by professional credibility. It is only by reading or listening to and objectively evaluating others' ideas that one can determine whether they are worthy of consideration. Two, the inclusion of such viewpoints encourages the important critical thinking skill of objectively evaluating an author's credentials and bias. This evaluation will illuminate an author's reasons for taking a particular stance on an issue and will aid in readers' evaluation of the author's ideas.

It is our hope that these books will give readers a deeper understanding of the issues debated and an appreciation of the complexity of even seemingly simple issues when good and honest people disagree. This awareness is particularly important in a democratic society such as ours in which people enter into public debate to determine the common good. Those with whom one disagrees should not be regarded as enemies but rather as people whose views deserve careful examination and may shed light on one's own.

Thomas Jefferson once said that "difference of opinion leads to inquiry, and inquiry to truth." Jefferson, a broadly educated man, argued that "if a nation expects to be ignorant and free . . . it expects what never was and never will be." As individuals and as a nation, it is imperative that we consider the opinions of others and examine them with skill and discernment. The Opposing Viewpoints series is intended to help readers achieve this goal.

David L. Bender and Bruno Leone,
Founders

Introduction

> *"Chinese parents believe that they know what is best for their children and therefore override all of their children's own desires and preferences. That's why Chinese daughters can't have boyfriends in high school and why Chinese kids can't go to sleepaway camp."*
>
> —*Amy Chua,*
> *"Why Chinese Mothers Are Superior,"*
> Wall Street Journal, *January 8, 2011.*

America is home to people from many different racial, ethnic, and national backgrounds. Different groups adapt to this diversity in different ways. In particular, parents and families have different approaches to raising their children.

These issues were highlighted when Amy Chua, a Yale Law School professor, printed an excerpt from her book *Battle Hymn of the Tiger Mother* as an op-ed in the January 8, 2011, *Wall Street Journal*. Chua, the mother of two daughters, argued that Chinese parents like herself managed to raise "such stereotypically successful kids" through strict rules and high expectations. Chua said her own children had never been allowed playdates, had not been allowed to watch TV, had not been allowed to get a grade less than A, and had been required to learn the piano and the violin. Chua argued that "Western parents try to respect their children's individuality, encouraging them to pursue their true passions, supporting their choices, and providing positive reinforcement and a nurturing environment. By contrast, the Chinese believe that the best way to protect their children is by preparing them for the future, letting them see what they're capable of, and arming them with skills, work habits and inner confidence that no one can ever take away."

Chua's article generated a large amount of controversy and numerous responses. For example, Jennifer Chang, writing in the *New York Times*, expressed concerns about Chua's "extreme parenting approach." She worried that such parenting "forces children to strive to meet their parents' preferences and goals—without knowing why they are doing what they do." She also noted that "extreme parenting seems to embrace a very narrow definition of what success means." Chang said that her own parents' rigid discipline in China did not lead her to success. Instead, she said, she only "started to excel when I had to make more of my own choices."

C.N. Le, a sociology professor at the University of Massachusetts, Amherst, had a lengthy and ambivalent reaction to Chua's article on his blog, *The Color Line*. He noted, first of all, that Chua's parenting style was probably in part a natural and positive reaction to belonging to a minority culture in the United States. Le argues that "many Asian and Asian American parents also understand that as a racial minority in American society, almost by necessity, they need to push their children a little further to make sure that they are able to overcome some of the hurdles and barriers that stand in our way." Le also suggested that some of the angry reactions to Chua—including death threats—were prompted by anxieties about growing Chinese world power and general anti-Asian sentiments. Thus, he concluded, the reactions to Chua demonstrated the racial animus that required her (in Le's view) to adopt her parenting style in the first place.

On the other hand, Le points out that strict parenting has had serious repercussions in the Asian American community. "[I]t is well worth repeating that Asian American women between 15–24 years old have the highest suicide rates of any racial, ethnic, age, and gender group in the U.S." He also argues that Chua draws too sharp a distinction between Chinese and Western parenting methods, suggesting that "many Chinese Americans and Asian American parents do both"—that is, they both demand success and give their children freedom and independence.

Chua's daughter, Sophia Chua-Rubenfeld, responded to her mother's essay, and to the controversy surrounding it, in a January 18, 2011, article in the *New York Post*. In her article, Chua-Rubenfeld, addressing her mother directly, noted, "A lot of people have accused you of producing robot kids who can't think for themselves. . . . I came to the opposite conclusion: I think your strict parenting forced me to be more independent. Early on, I decided to be an easy child to raise . . . but I also decided to be who I want to be." She further argued that her mother's determination and drive expanded her learning opportunities and forced Chua-Rubenfeld herself to live her life "at 110 percent."

The remainder of this book focuses on different aspects of interracial America in chapters titled *How Does Society View Interracial Relationships? What Impact Does Immigration Have on Interracial America? What Policies Promote Opportunities for People of All Races?* and *Is America Becoming a Post-Racial Society?* As in the argument over the tiger mother, the viewpoints in this book address issues of race, ethnicity, family, prejudice, and integration.

OPPOSING
VIEWPOINTS®
SERIES

CHAPTER 1

How Does Society View Interracial Relationships?

Chapter Preface

Today it is taken for granted that people of different racial backgrounds can marry. Until relatively recently, however, such marriages were outlawed in many parts of the United States under antimiscegenation (anti-interracial marriage) laws. For instance, in Arkansas, as the civil rights movement gained momentum, the legislature responded with harsher restrictions on blacks, including laws that penalized "people convicted of having interracial relationships. The penalty for a first conviction was a fine of $20 to $100. Second convictions subjected individuals to a $100 fine and up to a year in prison. Third and subsequent convictions would result in one to three years in prison," according to the 2008 article "Anti-Miscegenation Laws" by Charles F. Robinson II in *The Encyclopedia of Arkansas History & Culture.*

Two people affected by antimiscegenation laws were Richard Loving and Mildred Jeter. The two lived in a rural, integrated area of Virginia, where interracial couples were common. These couples, however, could not legally marry. Nonetheless, Richard, who was white, and Mildred, who was black, insisted on being joined legally. "In 1958, they went to Washington, D.C.—where interracial marriage was legal—to get married. But when they returned home, they were arrested, jailed and banished from the state for 25 years for violating the state's Racial Integrity Act," according to a June 11, 2007, article on NPR.org.

Richard and Mildred moved to Washington, D.C., for five years, but they longed to return to Virginia and their families. With the help of the American Civil Liberties Union, they brought a suit against the state of Virginia. After several years, their case reached the US Supreme Court. Before that Court, the Lovings' lawyer, Bernard Cohen, argued,

The Lovings have the right to go to sleep at night knowing that if should they not wake in the morning, their children would have the right to inherit from them. They have the right to be secure in knowing that, if they go to sleep and do not wake in the morning, that one of them, a survivor of them, has the right to Social Security benefits. All of these are denied to them, and they will not be denied to them if the whole anti-miscegenistic scheme of Virginia is found unconstitutional.

The Court agreed with Cohen and, on June 12, 1967, struck down Virginia's antimiscegenation law. "The fifteen remaining state miscegenation laws were also voided, and the Loving family moved back to Central Point," according to a February 23, 2011, post on the *Persephone Magazine* blog.

Richard Loving died in a car crash in 1975. Mildred rarely spoke publically, but she did release a statement in 2007 on the fortieth anniversary of the ruling, in which she explicitly linked the right of interracial marriage to the right of gay marriage. She said,

Surrounded as I am now by wonderful children and grand-children, not a day goes by that I don't think of Richard and our love, our right to marry, and how much it meant to me to have that freedom to marry the person precious to me, even if others thought he was the "wrong kind of person" for me to marry. I believe all Americans, no matter their race, no matter their sex, no matter their sexual orientation, should have that same freedom to marry. Government has no business imposing some people's religious beliefs over others. Especially if it denies people's civil rights. I am still not a political person, but I am proud that Richard's and my name is on a court case that can help reinforce the love, the commitment, the fairness, and the family that so many people, black or white, young or old, gay or straight seek in life. I support the freedom to marry for all.

The following viewpoints will look at issues and controversies surrounding interracial marriages and interracial families.

"Most Americans say they approve of interracial marriage, with more than 6 in 10 saying they're OK if a family member marries outside his or her group."

Interracial Marriage Is Increasingly Common

Husna Haq

Husna Haq is a senior editor at the Islamic Monthly *and a correspondent for* Christian Science Monitor, National Geographic, *and other publications. In the following viewpoint, she reports that interracial marriage and approval of interracial marriage have increased substantially over the last several decades. Haq notes that rates of intermarriage among whites and blacks especially have increased. Asians and Hispanics are less likely to marry someone whose ethnic background is different from their own, as high levels of immigration have given these groups more opportunities to marry within their communities. Haq concludes by noting that intermarriage is higher among black men than it is for black women. Asian women, however, are more likely to marry outside their ethnicity than Asian men.*

As you read, consider the following questions:

1. How did the interracial marriage rate in 2008 compare with the rates in the 1960s and the 1980s?

2. According to Jeffrey Passel, what evidence suggests that changes in attitudes toward interracial marriage are a generational phenomenon?

3. What is the reason for high rates of intermarriage among black men and Asian women, according to Daniel Lichter?

Americans are more likely than ever before to marry outside their race or ethnicity.

Americans Approve of Interracial Marriage

Nearly 1 in 7 marriages in 2008 was interracial or interethnic, according to a report released by the Pew Research Center Friday [2010]. That's more than double the intermarriage rate of the 1980s and six times the intermarriage rate of the 1960s.

Also, most Americans say they approve of interracial marriage, with more than 6 in 10 saying they're OK if a family member marries outside his or her group. Thirty-five percent say they already have a family member who is married to someone of a different race or ethnicity.

"Race relations have certainly changed in a positive way," says Daniel Lichter, a professor of sociology at Cornell University in Ithaca, N.Y. "This indicates greater racial tolerance, a blurring of the racial divides in the US. In general, it's an optimistic report."

Still, he cautions against notions that the United States is entering a postracial era.

"I don't think these racial boundaries are going to go away anytime soon, despite these patterns we're seeing over past 20 years," Dr. Lichter says. "It's hard to imagine the black-white divide in particular is going to go away anytime soon."

Waves of immigrants from Latin America and Asia are driving the intermarriage trend by enlarging the pool of potential marriage partners, says Jeffrey Passel, a lead researcher and author of Pew's report.

"American society is becoming more diverse, and workplaces, schools, and other arenas are fairly open so people can meet others of different races on one-to-one levels," Mr. Passel says. "Underneath that, there's a broad acceptance of interracial marriages that 40 or 50 years ago just didn't exist."

But, he adds, "It's very much a generational phenomenon." While 80 to 90 percent of people under age 30 say they find interracial marriages acceptable, that number falls to about 30 percent for those over 65, he says. "People 65 and over grew up in the '30s, '40s, and '50s when such things weren't acceptable or were illegal. That's an indicator of how things have changed."

Rates of Intermarriage Are Rising for Whites and Blacks

Approximately 280,000 of the roughly 2 million marriages in 2008 were between spouses of different races or ethnicities, according to the Pew report. White-Hispanic couplings accounted for the greatest proportion of those intermarriages, at 41 percent. White-Asian couples made up 15 percent, and white-black couples 11 percent.

The report found vastly different rates of intermarriage for each of the groups studied. Among all newlyweds in 2008, 9 percent of whites, 16 percent of blacks, 26 percent of Hispanics, and 31 percent of Asians married someone whose race or ethnicity was different from their own.

But while blacks nearly tripled their intermarriage rates from 1980, and whites more than doubled theirs, the rates have hardly changed for Hispanics and Asians over the past 30 years.

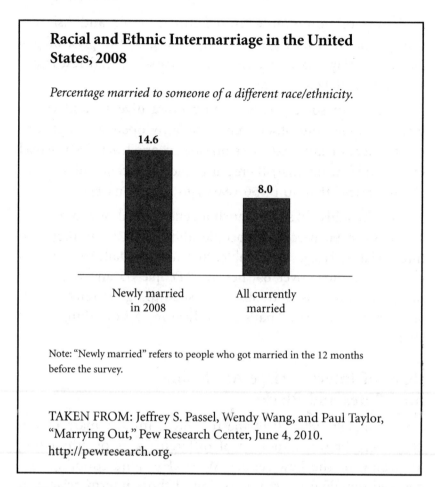

Racial and Ethnic Intermarriage in the United States, 2008

Percentage married to someone of a different race/ethnicity.

Note: "Newly married" refers to people who got married in the 12 months before the survey.

TAKEN FROM: Jeffrey S. Passel, Wendy Wang, and Paul Taylor, "Marrying Out," Pew Research Center, June 4, 2010. http://pewresearch.org.

"For whites and blacks, new [Asian and Hispanic] immigrants and their now grown US-born children have enlarged the pool of potential partners for marrying outside one's own racial or ethnic group," Passel writes in the Pew report. "But for Hispanics and Asians, the ongoing immigration wave has greatly enlarged the pool of potential partners for in-group marrying."

Lichter of Cornell has documented this trend in his own research. In some cases, he says, immigration is reinforcing cultural and ancestral identities.

"Native-born populations are returning to their national-origin group, in part through marriage," he says. "An increasing share of second-generation Hispanics are marrying first-generation immigrants. If marriage is one factor of assimilation, this represents a slowdown in assimilation among Asians and Hispanics."

The report also tracks stark differences in intermarriage by gender.

Some 22 percent of black male newlyweds in 2008 married outside their race, compared with just 9 percent of black female newlyweds.

Among Asians, it's an opposite pattern. Some 40 percent of Asian female newlyweds in 2008 married outside their race, compared with just 20 percent of Asian male newlyweds.

"A lot of this has to do with cultural definitions of beauty and stereotypes of gender roles . . . the exotic Asian woman and the patriarchal man," Lichter says.

This can also create tension within racial and ethnic communities.

"The opportunities to marry for African American women are exacerbated by high shares of black men marrying out, combined with extraordinarily high rates of incarceration among black men and higher rates of mortality," says Lichter. "That leads to a shortage of men to marry in the black community."

"Interracial images are used to perpetuate negative stereotypes yet are simultaneously marketed as an example of
how color-blind we have become and of
the declining significance of race."

Interracial Couples Are Still Seen as Deviant

Erica Chito Childs

Erica Chito Childs is a professor of sociology at Hunter College
and the City University of New York Graduate College. In the
following viewpoint, she argues that images of interracial couples
in popular culture continue to portray those couples as deviant.
Interracial couples, she says, are shown as odd, or dangerous, or
else are used to show the color-blindness and virtue of whites.
She concludes that interracial images in the media promote
negative stereotypes. She also argues that interracial couples in
real life continue to confront negative stereotypes and racism
from friends, relatives, and strangers due to the way minorities
are portrayed in the media.

As you read, consider the following questions:

1. According to Childs, for what two reasons are interracial relationships still depicted even though they are widely opposed by whites?

2. Who does Childs say controls media and popular culture?

3. What factors affect the experience of Latinas/os according to Childs?

Traveling through the worlds of television, film, media coverage, Internet, and music, it is clear that certain stories about interracial sex and relationships are retold in a limited number of ways. If these stories were nothing more than entertainment, and the images had no significance in our everyday lives, then we wouldn't need to be concerned. Yet unfortunately, these images influence how individuals interact with one another in the larger society and reflect existing racial inequalities. Whites have been simultaneously appalled and intrigued, offended and attracted to racial Others sexually, while monitoring, disciplining, and indulging, and this hasn't changed. . . .

Interracial Sex Sells and Alienates

Throughout the various media realms—television, film, news media, and the less clearly defined intersecting worlds of music, sports, and youth culture—representations of interracial sex and relationships follow certain patterns, and what emerges is a delicate dance between interracial sex sells and interracial sex alienates. The small number of representations as well as the particular types of depictions of interracial relationships, when they are shown, reveals the lingering opposition to interracial sexuality and marriage as well as the persistent racialized images of racial Others and the protection of whiteness. Interracial representations are symbolic struggles over meaning, not only in how interracial relationships are portrayed but also in how they are received, understood, and responded to in the larger society. In particular, interracial images are used to perpetuate negative stereotypes yet are simultaneously marketed as an example of how color-blind we have become and of the declining significance of race. Yet one may ask, Why are interracial relationships shown at all if they are still widely opposed by whites and other racial groups? The answer is twofold, . . . showing interracial relationships is a necessary piece of the current rhetoric that asserts race no longer matters and the representations are only shown in ways that either deviantize these relationships, privilege whiteness, or support the contention that America is color-blind. . . .

Deviant Relationships

This view of interracial relationships as deviant has existed throughout America's history; therefore, it is not surprising that most media and popular culture still depict interracial sexual relations as outside the realm of acceptable behavior.

Overwhelmingly, representations of interracial relationships reinforce the idea that these unions are problematic. These unions, if presented at all, are part of marginal story lines rather than centered. Moreover, there are virtually no films that include a happily partnered interracial couple or interracial wedding within the context of a stable, middle-class world. Through these cultural images, interracial relationships between whites and nonwhites are most often constructed as deviant, undoubtedly because these unions are still unacceptable to large numbers of whites.

The deviant nature of interracial relationships is reinforced in various ways. They are invisible, as evidenced in how rarely we see interracial couples on television or film, particularly men of color with white women. In the media, black and Latino victims are less likely to be acknowledged or believed, and as we saw in the differential coverage between the Central

Park jogger and the Tawana Brawley case or the Kobe Bryant and Duke University lacrosse team rape allegations,[1] the media tends to ignore or misrepresent women of color who allege they are victims of sexual assault by white men. Another way they are rendered deviant is by portraying the relationships as taboo, used in television and film to provide added comedy, mockery, tragedy, suspense, or a temporary distraction to the real plotline because the interracial relationship is outside the norm. In many films, the interracial relationship is the symbol of a downward spiral and deviant world, particularly if it involves a white woman with a man of color. Also deviant, interracial relationships are presented as a fantasy or fetish through a make-believe world, a dream sequence, a temporary crush, or a rendezvous in an exotic locale that allows the viewer to dabble in difference, living vicariously through the characters: this happens most in representations of women of color on television who only desire white men like on *Friends* and *ER*, or with film actresses like Halle Berry, Thandie Newton, and Jennifer Lopez, who are mostly paired opposite white men. Since those who produce the images are interested in making money, they will produce images that sell, which reveals the fine line between having diverse casts that may attract the maximum number of viewers because they appeal to all racial groups and losing viewers because of the diverse mix. Those who track how much money a film will gross, such as Robert Bucksbaum, president of the company Reel Source Inc., argue that "money is the driving force behind interracial couples in film," the relative lack of depictions may signal otherwise or, based on what images appear, depicting deviant interracial relationships is the moneymaker. . . .

1. Tawana Brawley was a black fifteen-year-old who alleged that she was raped by six white men in 1987; the Central Park jogger was a white woman who was raped in 1989; Kobe Bryant was a black basketball star accused of rape in 2003; three members of the Duke Lacrosse team were accused of raping a black woman in 2006.

The Purpose of Interracial Media Images

If interracial unions are continuously constructed as outside the norm, who creates the images and what purposes do they serve? . . . By constructing interracial relationships as a deviation from the norm, it is not only a means of privileging same-race unions, but also, more importantly, it is a way of perpetuating ideas about racial difference, white superiority, and racial stereotypes. Most stories involving an interracial union depict whites as progressive and good, like television's Dr. Carter on *ER* and Amy Gray on *Judging Amy*, or in films like *Bulworth*, *The Bodyguard*, *Fools Rush In*, *Monster's Ball*, and *Something New*, yet still the dangers of interracial intimacy are clear. Casting interracial relationships does not change the racial images that exist, but instead it works as "part of a broader program of hegemonic recuperation, a program that has at its main focus the reconstruction of white masculine power." For example, the relationship between a white man and woman of color is acceptable as long as the white man saves her and her world or the woman comes to his world, either symbolically through a transformation, like Jennifer Lopez's character who goes from a maid to a business executive, or geographically, by moving into his house or country. Yet if a white woman is paired interracially, most often it occurs in a deviant setting, where it causes problems and/or is met with opposition, usually from communities of color who are used to symbolically represent the potential problems that interracial intimacy causes. Not showing, deviantizing, or creating very unique exceptions of interracial relationships between whites and persons of color serves to reinforce the dominance of whiteness, and white masculinity, in particular. What emerges is how the gaze of the film is white male, and these depictions of interracial sex are white male fantasies that construct white masculinity in certain ways while reinforcing certain representations of people of color, and even white women. The interracial relationships we see and hear do not challenge racial boundaries, but rather happen securely within the constructed borders, such as a black woman in an all-white world or an interracial nonwhite relationship. By showing images of deviance, the racial hierarchy is not challenged; rather, it is arguably strengthened. . . .

Media and popular culture is still overwhelmingly controlled by whites, in particular a small group of white men, and the representations of interracial sex and couples created emerge out of their everyday realities, experiences, and fantasies: an integral part of racial ideology is "a substantive set of ideas and notions defending white power and privilege as meritorious and natural and accenting the alleged superiority of whites and the inferiority of those who are racially oppressed." In our contemporary world, the issue of power can never be overemphasized in terms of who creates the images, determines the discourses that prevail, and ultimately constructs the framework we watch and live in. While there are no longer public lynchings or laws denying racial groups full rights, the representations discussed serve similar purposes. These stories about interracial sex that are told in communities, in the media, and in popular culture are an integral part of the contemporary racist framework because they rationalize and legitimize white oppression of blacks and other racial minorities. This is achieved through presenting interracial couples as deviant, privileging and promoting whiteness, and strategically using interracial relationships to simultaneously deny race matters while perpetuating racial inequalities.

In both popular culture and real life, interracial couples are embraced under very specific circumstances and otherwise merely tolerated. In recent studies on the experiences of interracial couples, they tell stories of "supportive" families who make racist comments or won't allow their own children to marry interracially. Furthermore, white communities report that they "do not have a problem with interracial relationships but . . ." followed by a laundry list of reasons why they or their family shouldn't, couldn't, and wouldn't marry outside their race, particularly in relation to African Americans. Qualitative studies also document how even interracial couples report racialized thinking about their partners or the racial groups they come from. Representations of interracial sex and relationships allow for whites to maintain the myth of color blindness because, as Patricia Hill Collins argues, to be color-blind we need to see color, or more accurately, color safely contained. These representations include racialized comments and symbolic images of difference while promoting the notion of color blindness by placing outright opposition and racial prejudice as existing with an extreme racist group or bigoted individual. What is most dangerous about contemporary images is that they pass as positive proof that racism no longer exists while still delivering only particular derogatory views of interracial sexuality, and more importantly, damaging stereotypes of African American, Latinas/os, and Asian Americans, which allow white communities' and other racial communities' coded, racialized thoughts and actions to go unchallenged. This widespread use of nonracial and coded language masks contemporary racism and prejudice to the point where the representations are actually used as proof that racism is no longer a problem.

Stereotypes Persist

The representations of interracial unions also mirror the different racial positions that groups occupy in society. The experiences of Latinas/os vary greatly based on many factors such as ethnicity, skin color, and socioeconomic class status, similar to how Latina actresses like Jennifer Lopez's characters fluctuate. The traits and stories associated with the "Latina Lopez" as opposed to white Jennifer reveal how Latinas are represented in certain ways, but certain Latinas like Lopez have the ability to, at least temporarily, leave behind these representations. For Asian Americans, while still considered the

Interracial Relationships Remain Problematic

A major piece of my analysis involves the language whites use when discussing their views on interracial relationships, especially the way color is described as insignificant. Any issues concerning black-white unions that whites may have are often articulated in a color-blind discourse that deemphasizes race though the very rea son people make these statements is because skin color and race do matter, often most to those who espouse this color-blind discourse. Interracial relationships in particular and blacks in general are outside white groups' social worlds. And for those white partners of black-white couples, the response of their families and communities illustrate just how problematic these relationships still are when they occur within one's family or community.

Erica Chito Childs,
Navigating Interracial Borders:
Black-White Couples and Their Social Worlds.
New Brunswick, NJ: Rutgers University Press, 2005, p. 45.

model minority, Asian men and women are often relegated to service positions and mocked for their perceived language and cultural differences. The increasing number of marriages between white men and Asian women combined with the extremely low numbers of marriage between white women and Asian men can be understood at least partially through the different images. Illustrating the direct connection, one study of Asian-white couples found that these individuals often embrace the racialized stereotypes that dominate interracial representations, with Asian American men struggling with feeling inferior and being perceived as less masculine by Asian American women while white men with Asian women embrace the image of the Lotus Blossom: "Asian American women enforce Eurocentric gender ideology when they accept the objectification and feminization of Asian men and the parallel construction of white men as the most desirable sexual and marital partners." For black Americans, on various societal indicators in terms of education, employment, health, income, and marriage, blacks as a group lag behind whites and other racial groups. Not surprisingly, rates of marriage between blacks and whites remain low, while racism against blacks remains strongest among all racial groups. Undoubtedly, the dominant images we see of dangerous black men and sexually available black women contribute to this antiblack racism that permeates all realms of society, such as education, work, health, and wealth. Furthermore, when blacks are accused or believed to have committed an "interracial crime," they will be (per)prosecuted harder, but their immediate community, and to an extent the entire black race, also comes under scrutiny. When black women are the victims of rape, particularly by whites, their story seems to be quickly doubted by both the criminal/legal system, and the media passes on this doubt. Yet for whites, accusations of a crime that involves interracial sex can actually serve as an excuse such as in the Yusef Hawkins murder[2] or make it less likely the "crime" will be believed. By using the Kobe Bryant case (or O. J. [Simpson] trial) [both of which involved black celebrities who were acquitted] to argue whether or not race matters, it makes it easier for whites to affirm that race no longer matters, especially since the media pays little or no attention to the unknown black men who have been falsely accused or received stiffer penalties for crimes against white women—"the real racism that millions of people face every day is thus either too localized or generalized" and not the story that fits the white imagination. At the same

2. Yusef Hawkins was a black youth attacked and killed by a white gang in the New York Community of Bensonhurst in 1989.

time, the media lets pass under their radar stories that do not fit these molds, like the countless black women who are victims of rape or the interracial couples who are harassed by a group of white men. Just as whites as a group sit atop the racial hierarchy, there emerges a pattern that when whites are accused—white young men in the Yusef Hawkins case, the white Italian community of Bensonhurst, the white community of Vail, Colorado, during the Kobe Bryant case, and the white lacrosse players, Duke University, and Durham—the media participates in the protection of whiteness either through the characterization of those accused or the validation of the white communities. Through the media coverage, the protection and privileging of whiteness is clear. The representations of whites as a group remain positive, particularly in relation to characters of color. The problem of race is squarely placed with people of color, and the idea that all groups can be equally prejudiced is common without the acknowledgment of white racism.

Serving Majority Interests

These stories we hear and see are carefully constructed and serve specific purposes. Representations of interracial intimacy have less to do with how acceptable these unions are and more to do with whose interests are served. The media, like film and television, weave stories before the "story" is actually known, and how they decide to present the little bits of information they receive shows us the stories they assume to be true. These stories are based within a social structure that is organized on the idea of separate racial groups, with the accompanying ideology that there are distinct differences between the races: whites have produced this racial hierarchy and maintain it through continued separation, with a collective discourse against interracial unions being part of this. We see how the media approaches race as something that is played for a reason and manipulated for advantage, rarely acknowledging the extent to which race affects any interracial case. The reports are contradictory, where we hear that a white lawyer "playing the race card" carries more credibility, but we still hear from journalists that race does not matter and they "never think about race." The role of race is denied, yet people in Vail, Colorado, live in a area where there are virtually no black people, a popular sitcom like *Friends* can ignore the racial diversity of the city the show is set in [New York City], and we have darkened faces on magazine covers and Hangman T-shirts made of black athletes who have supposedly "transcended race." The fantasy of interracial relationships cannot be bogged down with the unpleasantness of racism, inequality, and discrimination, so it erases these structural and institutional realities that shape everyday social interaction.

> "I got tired of looking at every interracial couple then immediately thinking of my 'widdle' feelings. What the hell did these people have to do with me?"

Black Women Should Not Oppose Interracial Dating

Danielle Belton

Danielle Belton is a journalist who has written for publications including Essence Magazine, American Prospect, NPR, *and her own blog,* The Black Snob. *In the following viewpoint, she argues that black women should not be concerned about black men dating white women. Belton argues that interracial relationships are about the individuals in the relationship and should not be seen as political statements directed at other black women. Belton further suggests that worries about interracial dating are based in black women's self-esteem issues. She concludes that black women would do better to build their own self-confidence rather than worry about who is dating whom.*

As you read, consider the following questions:

1. What does Belton say caused her to stop caring about interracial dating?

2. According to Belton, why do black people in the United States often have self-esteem issues?

3. What does Belton say she would tell the two girls who jumped the white girl in the stairwell if she could go back in time?

A long crusty time ago in a high school far, far away there was an "epic" schoolyard fight over a boy, a black boy, who was dating a white girl who rode my bus. The exact reasons for the fisticuffs have been lost somewhat to history, but I vaguely recall that two black girls decided to take it upon themselves to "jump" the girl from my bus in the stairwell just before school let out.

Fighting over Interracial Dating

Perhaps one of the girls used to date the black boy. Perhaps some words had been spoken. But the fight was clearly over the boy and the gall of this particular white girl to date him. So they did confront her in the stairwell and shockingly, the white girl in question actually won the two-on-one fight.

I can still remember her elated face on the bus that afternoon as she talked about the fight in the most hyper voice possible, adrenaline still pumping. Her boyfriend was strangely proud and I was befuddled.

Mostly because I have always thought fighting over a boy, any boy, was dumb, even at 15. It hardly seemed worth it. And while, back then, I *thought* I understood why a couple of black girls would think it was a "beatdownable" offense for a white girl to date a black guy at our school, I knew the girl on the bus personally and she was a nice person.

I went years not thinking about the incident (which is why my memory of it is so crusty), but one day—and I can't remember when—I got tired of caring about interracial dating.

I got tired of ill-placed anger at strangers I didn't know. I got tired of looking at every interracial couple then immediately thinking of my "widdle" feelings. What the hell did these people have to do with me? It wasn't like they'd met, started dating and married just to personally ruin my day. The insecurity and anger was illogical. Especially considering most of the time I didn't actually want any of the men who had the white girlfriend or wife. I didn't even know them. It seemed like a waste of time because . . .

It wasn't about me.

I know plenty of black women (and black men to a lesser extent) who were amazingly militant about the whole black-white pairings and are prone to fly into some form of bitterness or rage as if every black-white coupling was a personal affront to their own self-worth. (See anything related to African American/Asian American [golf star] Tiger Woods.) Every couple became a moment of doubt to question themselves, then turn and question the couple. It was usually assumed the individual had "sold out" in some fashion or hated black people or themselves or both and [was] an awful person and that the white person, by association, was some smug interloper sent to make our lives miserable by stealing all the "good" black men from "us." That the interloper thought they were better than us and special because they had been chosen by this wayward Negro and so the self-hate train would ride into town.

Hate Is Easy

Of course, there was never any way to verify that these were the cases. They were mere assumptions based on what we'd heard or read or inferred or hoped was true. Because it's easier to say "He must hate all women like me" than say "I sometimes lack confidence because I have issues with how I look and feel." No one wants to openly admit to all those doubts of *maybe if I was more* (fill in the blank) *I would be better accepted, more desirable*. Hate spiral is MUCH easier and powerful. You can feel pretty energized after going on a good

Black Women Should Be Willing to Date Outside Their Race

So many black women are single, . . . says [writer Karyn Langhorne Folan], because they are stuck in the groove of a one-track song: sitting alone, waiting for that one "good" black man to come along and sweep them off their feet.

Waiting. Talking to girlfriends. Waiting. Going out alone. Waiting. Going to work. Waiting. . . .

Single black women with college degrees outnumber single black men with college degrees almost 3 to 1 in major urban areas such as Washington, according to a 2008 population survey by the U.S. Census Bureau. Given those numbers, any economist would advise them to start looking elsewhere.

DeNeen L. Brown,
"Single Black Women Being Urged to Date Outside Race,"
Washington Post, *February 25, 2010.*
www.washingtonpost.com.

rant about "no good, self-hating Negroes" and referring to all white women who date black men as "snowflake."

Black people, despite our best efforts, tend to have some self-esteem issues. For some it's worse than [for] others depending on what they had to personally endure. But it doesn't matter how light or dark you are, we all have to deal with some form of dreaded "Negro Derangement Syndrome" beset by growing up as a minority in a majority culture.

Part of that derangement is being routinely told via media and other black people that you are not good enough. Not light enough. Not pretty enough. Don't have Western features. Aren't the ideal beauty. With women, this is particularly devastating. Add to that fact that black women tend to be the most dogged about dating and marrying within their race, but are also the least likely to get married, the level of sexual jealousy is extremely high. Often to the point of being unbearable.

It was like everyone I knew was [actress] Angela Bassett and this was *Waiting to Exhale*[1] and "Git yo' shit" was the rallying cry. Everyone had a story of a slight, perceived or real, of abandonment by black men for white women. The most dramatic one I can recall was an old friend from my youth who was madly in love with a biracial man who identified himself as black, got her pregnant, but didn't want a child so she wound up having an abortion. They would later break up and he would later end up getting a white woman we both knew pregnant. She had the child and he sold his most prized possession, his expensive SUV, to buy a smaller car and his new girlfriend a car of her own.

My friend pretty much died inside, because as insulting as it was for him to have moved on from their relationship so quickly, he'd done it with a dreaded white girl. It made her put in doubt everything about their past relationship and her friends and enemies alike, latched on the white girl part rather than the "Your ex-boyfriend really sounds like an ass" part. Not that she helped it. For some sick reason she still wanted this man. Even though he'd proven to be not dependable and shallow. It was easy to focus on the white girl, who she didn't know very well and was not within our circle of friends, but it was her ex-boyfriend who'd hurt her. And because he was so shallow he was more than likely to move on and hurt his white girlfriend too (which he eventually did). The man she was crying and fighting over was HARDLY a prize, yet I saw how it destroyed her self-esteem.

---

1. *Waiting to Exhale* was a popular 1995 movie about the relationship troubles of black women. Angela Bassett was one of the stars.

Not About You

I tried to tell her that sometimes, it isn't about you. That his choices were about him and what he wanted. Her boyfriend treated her badly the whole time they were together. Why would she even want or care what he does? Let the white woman deal with his drama. I found it unlikely that the same guy who wanted one girl to get an abortion was going to be Mr. Liberated and Sensitive Man with the white girl. And he was just as much of a troglodyte with his new girlfriend as he was with the old. She just kept her baby.

She still got stuck with him. Horrible, no good him.

Yet the angst remained.

As an adult I knew black people who struggled with trusting blacks who'd married outside of their race, even if they were still very involved with the community. I befriended a pair of siblings who had both married white people, but were involved in mentoring black students. They loved their spouses and families, but talked about their own problems, like dealing with a daughter who was more drawn to identify with her white mother's side than her black father's because of the racism she'd experienced as a child. This bothered her father who wanted his daughter to be proud of being both white and black. They weren't self-loathing, self-hating black people. They were just black people who happened to have married white people. And they hadn't actively sought out to marry only white people. They just married people they could relate to. It didn't make any sense to despise or be judgmental of these couples who became my friends.

Because, again, it wasn't about me.

I'm not one who talks about interracial dating as the panacea to all the woes of single black women. I think it's weird when some folks go the full 180 and almost reduce it to a fetish, preaching to the gospel of "date a white man" with the same vigor as those who act like black women are embroiled in some dating war over black men. But then I'm not someone who feels the need to prove how down I am either by saying things like I'm so down that I don't even find lighter black people with Western features attractive. (A statement I will never quite get. I mean, you're so not attracted to white people you reject light-skinned black people too? Is that based on pre-rejection because you think the light-skinned people will reject you for being darker, and if so, isn't this another "it's not about you" scenario?)

Taking it personally doesn't help anyone. If someone dates someone outside of their race it was because they wanted to and not because something is inherently wrong with you (or them for that matter). Even if the person doing the dating outside of their race is of the type who bad-mouths other black people, that still has NOTHING TO DO WITH YOU. That's all about them and their own self-loathing.

If I could go back in time and talk to those two girls before they decided to jump the white girl in the stairwell, I would ask them why? Why would you fight over a boy who doesn't want you and why would you attack the girl when, again, it was the boy who chose her? Why would you risk getting kicked out of school just to stop the inevitable? Some black guys are going to date white girls. Attempting to beat up the white girls will not turn that tide. That boy didn't belong to you just because you shared the same pigmentation. He wasn't promised to you.

It's just not worth it.

People would be better served in building their own self-confidence rather than trying to control the uncontrollable. You'd be better off learning to love yourself than becoming mired in bitterness and hate over that thing that's not really about you. We all want to be loved and desired, but you're not going to get it if you're too worried about what *Becky and 'em* are doing with that black guy over there.

> "As a black woman who has been in-
> volved with a white guy for more than
> a year, I've faced my fair share of hos-
> tility from white women, and some
> Asian ones, who seem resentful of my
> partnership."

Black Women Are Too Often Singled Out as the Ones Who Oppose Interracial Dating

Nadra Kareem

*Nadra Kareem is a journalist and writer whose work has ap-
peared in publications including the* Los Angeles Times, Santa
Fe Reporter, L.A. Watts Times, *and About.com. In the following
viewpoint, she notes that black women are often unfairly charged
with being the main group opposed to interracial dating. Kareem argues that, in her own experience dating a white man, she
has found that white women are often hostile to interracial
couples. She suggests that white women may be uncomfortable
acknowledging black women as social equals or competitors.*

As you read, consider the following questions:

1. In what ways does Kareem say white women have shown their hostility to her relationship with a white man?

2. According to Kareem, how are the objections of white women to interracial relationships different from the objections of black women?

3. What does Kareem argue may be part of the reason for the success of talk show host Oprah Winfrey with white women?

Do black women regard interracial relationships as a personal affront?

Hostility from Whites

I can't count the number of times I've seen this issue raised. On June 2 [2009], it surfaced once more when blogger the Black Snob [author Danielle Belton] posted a thought-provoking piece on those who oppose interracial relationships called "Sometimes the White Girl (Or Guy) Isn't About You (Unconventional Wisdom)."

The post begins with the Snob recalling her days in school when two black girls unsuccessfully try to jump a white classmate who's dating a black guy. Throughout the piece, the Snob not only questions the rationale the two girls used to justify beating up their white peer but the rationale that black women in general draw upon to oppose interracial relationships. Are black women being fair when they assume that a black guy dating a white chick is a sell-out? And how do the insecurities of black women in Western society factor into their objection of interracial relationships?

She writes, "Some black guys are going to date white girls. Attempting to beat up the white girls will not turn that tide. . . . You'd be better off learning to love yourself than becoming mired in bitterness and hate over that thing that's not really about you."

The Snob's points are valid. However, after reading her piece and others like it, I find myself wondering why black women are constantly portrayed as if they are the only ones who react negatively to interracial relationships. As a black woman who has been involved with a white guy for more than a year, I've faced my fair share of hostility from white women, and some Asian ones, who seem resentful of my partnership. None of these women have disapproved of my relationship aloud, but they don't really have to. Their body language says enough.

They do double takes when they learn my boyfriend and I are together. They give me the side-eye or attempt to look me up and down when they think I won't notice. Others have just been aloof or exhibited general bitchiness when I tried to make conversation with them. I know that if I am having such experiences, other black women involved with non-black men are as well. Yet, black women continue to bear the onus for the hostility that black-white interracial couples face.

White Women May Be Threatened

The sad thing about this to me is that the reasons a black woman might object to an interracial relationship are wholly different from the reasons a white woman might. Black women worry how the black community will be affected overall if, say, the most successful black men find themselves with white women again and again. They worry about the effect interracial relationships have on low marriage rates in the black community. In contrast, when I encounter white women who cop an attitude upon discovering that my boyfriend and I are an item, their hostility comes from a very different place—a place of superiority.

It's as if they are asking themselves, "Why on earth would he be with a black girl when I'm here?" Adding insult to injury is that it doesn't seem to matter whether I'm more or less physically attractive than these women. That I'm black alone makes me inferior in their eyes. It comes down to this: women accustomed to being prizes in Western society are thrown for a loop when they see a white man who's chosen a different option. As ridiculous as it sounds, their behavior reminds me of the Valley girl at the beginning of the "Baby Got Back" record [by Sir Mix-a-Lot] who says in disgust, "She's so *black*." Black women aren't supposed to be desirable, so when an eligible white male partners with a black woman, it's not surprising that some people are going to react with shock or hostility.

I discussed this issue with a black friend several months ago. Then, she said of white women, "You know they're threatened by us."

Sure, I know that some white women may be intimidated by black women they view in stereotypes—loud, overbearing and aggressive. But I did not think that white women were threatened by black women in the romantic realm. Is this akin to white men being jealous of the fabled size of black men's penises? Are white women worried that they can't compete with black women sexually? I don't know. Yet, this isn't the first time I've seen this issue raised. Years ago when I was reading a profile on Oprah Winfrey, the writer suggested that the talk show queen wouldn't have so many white women fans if she were more sexually threatening. In short, if Oprah were slender and alluring instead of the woman white ladies bring their problems to, she wouldn't be as successful.

I wonder how valid this statement is. I do know that, on the surface, a few of the hostile white women I've encountered have no problem with black women. They do volunteer work involving the black community and are eager to sympathize with the woes of black women. But, upon learning that my boyfriend chose to date me, they are taken aback. Rather than being a rung below them on the social ladder—someone in need of their help—a black woman had effectively become their competitor and, thus, their equal.

> *"Rather than being a source of conflict, therefore, the biracial nature of the family may represent a source of advantage."*

Children of Interracial Parents Benefit

Simon Cheng and Brian Powell

Simon Cheng is a sociologist at the University of Connecticut; Brian Powell is a sociologist at Indiana University. In the following viewpoint, they report on research indicating that biracial families generally provide more resources for their children than monoracial families do. The authors also note that biracial children may face some problems with discrimination and suggest the families may invest more in the children to compensate. The authors also point out, however, that black men/white women biracial couples seem to invest fewer resources in their children than comparable monoracial couples.

As you read, consider the following questions:

1. According to the authors, children of biracial couples have more of an advantage in economic and cultural resources than they do in what kinds of resources?

Simon Cheng and Brian Powell, "Under and Beyond Constraints: Resource Allocation to Young Children from Biracial Families," *American Journal of Sociology*, vol. 112, no. 4, January 2007, pp. 1080–1082. Copyright © 2007 by Simon Cheng and Brian Powell. Reprinted by permission of the University of Chicago Press and the authors.

2. Why are the authors not surprised to find that biracial families differ from monoracial families?

3. Besides black father/white mother families, what other biracial pairings do the authors say on average invest relatively little in their children?

The recent increase in biracial families has not gone unnoticed by the sociological community, but empirical analyses of the biracial population typically have emphasized either factors spurring racial exogamy or issues concerning the identity formation of biracial youths. Some researchers have speculated that biracial families may disadvantage their offspring because of the complex family dynamics and various structural impediments faced by interracial couples. Studies of family, education, and racial stratification, however, have rarely considered the differences between biracial and monoracial families in their parenting practices. In this study, we demonstrate that, although biracial families differ by the sex/race compositions of interracial couples, an overall more positive portrayal may be warranted, at least in the area of parental resource allocations.

Biracial Families Invest More in Their Children

Our study offers evidence that biracial families on average post an advantageous educational investment profile over their associated monoracial families. This biracial advantage, however, is contingent upon the types of familial resources and interracial pairings. Once the pancategory of biracial families is disaggregated into more detailed configurations of biracial families, it becomes clear that children of black father/white mother households are the only biracial group that is more disadvantaged than their corresponding monoracial peers. With this notable exception, resources provided by parents from biracial families typically exceed those offered by

Summary of Differences in Cultural Capital Investments Between Biracial and Monoracial Families

Racial Categories

Subgrouped by gender:

White father and black mother

Reading-related cultural activities	Higher
Nonreading cultural activities	NS
Participate in art class/lesson	NS
Visit cultural settings	Higher

Black father and white mother

Reading-related cultural activities	Higher
Nonreading cultural activities	NS
Participate in art class/lesson	NS
Visit cultural settings	NS

White father and Hispanic mother

Reading-related cultural activities	Higher
Nonreading cultural activities	Higher
Participate in art class/lesson	NS
Visit cultural settings	Higher

Hispanic father and white mother

Reading-related cultural activities	Higher
Nonreading cultural activities	Higher
Participate in art class/lesson	NS
Visit cultural settings	NS

White father and Asian mother

Reading-related cultural activities	Higher
Nonreading cultural activities	Middle
Participate in art class/lesson	Higher
Visit cultural settings	NS

Asian father and white mother

Reading-related cultural activities	NS
Nonreading cultural activities	Middle
Participate in art class/lesson	Higher
Visit cultural settings	NS

[CONTINUED]

Summary of Differences in Cultural Capital Investments Between Biracial and Monoracial Families

Racial Categories	
Subgrouped by gender:	
White father and other mother	
Reading-related cultural activities	NS
Nonreading cultural activities	NS
Participate in art class/lesson	NS
Visit cultural settings	NS
Other father and white mother	
Reading-related cultural activities	Higher
Nonreading cultural activities	Higher
Participate in art class/lesson	NS
Visit cultural settings	Higher
No gender subgroup:	
Black and Hispanic	
Reading-related cultural activities	NS
Nonreading cultural activities	Higher
Participate in art class/lesson	NS
Visit cultural settings	NS
Hispanic and Asian	
Reading-related cultural activities	NS
Nonreading cultural activities	Higher
Participate in art class/lesson	NS
Visit cultural settings	NS

Note: Biracial families were compared to two groups of monoracial families. Codes for reading the table are as follows: NS = racial differences are not significant. Higher = higher parental investments than both monoracial groups. Middle = closer to the monoracial group with higher parental investments. Lower = lower parental investments than both monoracial groups.

TAKEN FROM: Simon Cheng and Brian Powell, "Under and Beyond Constraints: Resource Allocation to Young Children from Biracial Families," *American Journal of Sociology*, vol.112, no. 4, January 2007, pp. 1073–1074.

parents from one or both of the corresponding monoracial groups. This advantageous profile in parental investments to children is more applicable for economic and cultural resources than for interactional/social ones. Regarding the sex differences of interracial couples, our analyses suggest that black father/white mother, Hispanic father/white mother, and white father/other mother families tend to invest less in their children than interracial families with opposite sex/race compositions.

Since scholars have documented the import of race in virtually every aspect of social life, it is not surprising that we find significant differences between biracial and monoracial families; however, the direction of these patterns may well be unanticipated. In this study, we contend that biracial families' resource allocations to their children's education can be conceptualized as a function of social constraints and human agency. Under this premise, we observe that biracial families often show greater investments in their children than one or both monoracial groups. This suggests that parents may exercise their human agency to go beyond the influences of interracial constraints. Certainly, it is possible that individuals who choose to enter an interracial marriage are qualitatively different than those who enter a monoracial one. If so, this difference goes beyond sociodemographic ones, for the pattern holds even with admittedly imperfect controls for education, income, and other factors. An alternative or addition to this selectivity argument is that interracial couples develop new behavioral patterns in order to compensate for their children's disadvantaged or marginalized social positions. In other words, parents from biracial families, cognizant of the disadvantages or marginality of their children in school settings, provide more resources to their children in order to compensate for their children's putative disadvantage. Rather than being a source of conflict, therefore, the biracial nature of the family may represent a source of advantage. We emphasize, however, that qualitative research focusing on interracial households may be required in order to more fully understand the dynamics of these parenting behaviors.

Some Challenges Facing Biracial Families

Our empirical findings also highlight several structural constraints that may impede biracial families' resource allocations to children's education. Three familial/social factors were identified in this study: conflicting preferences within the family, social disapproval against interracial families, and status inconsistency between interracial spouses. Of these, we found little support that conflicting values have a substantial negative influence on biracial families' parenting practices, for biracial families rarely show fewer educational investments than do monoracial families. We found, however, that parents from biracial families are less able to develop beneficial network ties than to allocate financial and cultural resources to their children. Since extrafamilial social resources are embedded in social relations, this finding suggests that stigmatization factors may constrain interracial parents' ability to mobilize resources beyond their families. Correspondingly, we also observe that black-biracial families experience difficulties connecting with their own parents, arguably due at least in part to the historical antagonism against intermarriage between black men and white women and against African Americans in general.

The lower investment of black father/white mother and, to a lesser extent, Hispanic father/white mother families than interracial families with opposite sex/race compositions provides some evidence that race/sex status inconsistency between interracial spouses presents additional challenges for minority man/white woman couples and further affects their investment in children's education. Together, the potential prejudice against black/white couples and race/sex status inconsistency offer an explanation for why black father/white mother families are the only interracial combination that shows a disadvantageous investment profile than both their monoracial and white father/black mother counterparts.

> *"The problem today is that White parents are raising their Black offspring using White paradigms of parenting, which are often antithetical to Black manhood."*

Children of Interracial Parents Face Special Difficulties

Frank A. Jones

Frank A. Jones is the publisher of Gibbs Magazine *and of the small-press publishing house Mirror-Gibbs Publications. In the following viewpoint, he argues that a white parent raising a biracial child, especially a biracial boy, faces special difficulties. Jones says that white parents assume white privilege; they treat their child as if he will not be discriminated against. Biracial children with one black parent generally appear black, however, which means they will face discrimination. Jones says biracial boys must learn discipline early to excel in the face of an unjust society.*

As you read, consider the following questions:

1. What does Jones say is the new aspect of biracial children?

2. How does Jones specifically define the notion of White Privilege?

3. What does Jones say a black perspective on black cultures is *not*?

Raising a biracial son who is Black and White can be difficult for some parents and the child; it can be even more difficult for a single White female raising a Black son alone.

The Difficulties Facing Black Male Children

There are many concerns that all parents should have as they raise their children, especially Black male children. This is because of the rigors the Black male will have to face in his life, and the influences that will pull on him.

After administering two treatment centers for delinquent males, and having worked closely with Black, White, Hispanic, and biracial children, I think I may know some of the difficulties of parenting these young men. In spite of the psychologists, social workers, staff, sophisticated tests, etc., what we were doing most of all in those treatment centers was providing parental guidance to children who had not received much of that.

One day we had to move a biracial youth from our Fairfield facility, predominantly White, to our Oakland facility, predominantly Black. The youth was terrified to go to Oakland. He kept saying, "I can't go to Oakland, Frank; look at me, I can't go there. I won't fit in." He was a biracial youth.

More was going on inside of him than being biracial; he was afraid of other Black males. But unless someone would have told us this child was biracial, we would not have noticed it in his looks—he looked like a million other brown-skinned Blacks in our society who think nothing of their complexion, other than knowing they are brown-skinned. This child, however, had something placed in him that made him feel he was different from other Blacks, and *that something is a problem in raising Black, biracial children.*

White Paradigms for Black Children

For years, Blacks and Whites have had sexual liaisons, whether legal or illegal, and those liaisons have bred biracial children—the Black descendants of Thomas Jefferson in the news represent just one famous case among many long-standing liaisons.

Consequently, and as a result, Blacks have accepted anyone as Black who claims to be Black. That is part of the reason for the vast diversity of hues among those who are considered African Americans.

The term biracial is new, but the type of child is not new among Blacks. The new aspect of biracial children is that they are being raised by their White parents, whereas in the past, especially in the South, they would have been aborted or put up for adoption.

The problem today is that White parents are raising their Black offspring using White paradigms of parenting, which are often antithetical to Black manhood, and when embedded in Black children, that paradigm, with all its assumptions of White Privilege usually not experienced by people of non-white hue, may cause them to behave as the young biracial ward of my center behaved when told that he would be moved to Oakland: he saw himself as different and the other Black males (without biracial parenting or lineage) as dangerous and threatening. When this notion is put into children, it alienates them from the Black part of their heritage and harms their socialization.

A child needs more than love to be raised successfully. The idea that, "*I just want to give my child love*," is nice, but it is an insufficient parenting methodology. Children need more than love because that which is defined as love is usually not love at all, but affection and often parent ego-gratification. Black children need guidance, discipline, self-perception, and a survival perspective to function in this society. A White person can deny the presence of White Privilege and other forms of White discrimination, but when parenting a biracial child, reality dispenses with those imaginations and failures to seek reality—their eyes become open to the fuller spectrum of American society. . . .

White Privilege

The male child in our treatment center had a notion placed within him at a very early age by his White mother, and she was probably unaware of her placing it in him; the notion of White Privilege—certain rights the child has that exist for him by virtue of his being White in America. Again, I repeat for emphasis, if a White American has not understood White Privilege, try parenting a Black male child and watch that child grow up in this society. No amount of the traditional White rationalization will obscure the ubiquity of White Privilege not experienced by that Black biracial child.

White Privilege in the head of a Black male is not a part of Black consciousness and is not placed in a Black child by Black parents. White parents raising Black or their own biracial children raise them from a perspective that is not Black but White. They see their biracial children as White and assume that they will have all of the bias privileges and experiences that Whites confer upon each other, but deny to non-Whites. Understandably, they don't want their children to suffer the pains of discrimination, low self-esteem, and the lack of privileges that most Blacks experience in this nation. No parent wants that for his/her child.

The White parent's desire is laudable, and it is the desire of every parent; it's a universal concept of parenting and love. But the problem is many White parents of biracial children do not see what this society has done to Black children, especially Black males, and what it continues to do. The White parents

The Importance of White Privilege

White privilege is the other side of racism. Unless we name it, we are in danger of wallowing in guilt or moral outrage with no idea of how to move beyond them. It is often easier to deplore racism and its effects than to take responsibility for the privileges some of us receive as a result of it. By choosing to look at white privilege, we gain an understanding of who benefits from racism, and how they do so. Once we understand how white privilege operates, we can begin to take steps to dismantle it on both a personal and an institutional level.

Paula S. Rothernberg, White Privilege:
Essential Readings on the Other Side of Racism.
New York: Worth Publishers, 208, p. 3.

of biracial children see their children as their White offspring; the outside world sees them only as *Black kids* with light skin; so the system that Whites have perfected to disadvantage Blacks and privilege themselves will be at work on these biracial children in spite of how their parents see them. And if these children have not learned to handle the systems of aggression that have been set up against the Black male, they will be made to confront it *brutishly* by the still predominately White police departments. And that system may throw them into disarray, depression, and even death.

Even today, White police *in many instances "see a wallet as a gun in the hands of a Black male."* This is the culture for many, a culture that even finds its way into some Black and Asian police, as the recent incident of Asian police brutality of a Black retired college counselor in San Mateo County indicates. This is a problem that White parents must grapple with in raising their biracial sons. . . .

The Child Should Be Raised as a Black Child

White parents cannot help their children by infusing them with the idea of White Privilege; other Whites do not respect it because they see these children as Black. Therefore, the White parent raising a biracial child, one who is Black/White, or the non-White parent raising a child who is Black/any-other-race should understand that Blacks normally dominate the color gene pool so that the child is perceptibly Black and not White. This is usually true with other races as well. And since this is true, the child should be raised as a Black child. Yes, he should respect all of his parentage, but as concerning his worldview, for that child to be successful, he needs to be raised to see himself as Black and have a Black perspective.

Do not misconstrue what a Black perspective or Black culture is; it is not what is shown on rap videos and classic Black stereo White media—those videos and media usually project the 27% underclass of Blacks, not the 73% of Blacks who are doing well and have no sense of the gansta rap mentality. Somehow, to the American mass, hideous stereotypes and caricatures of Blacks have greater fluency than real (the majority) Black life. A biracial child's perception of Black life and Black people should not be confused with the warped stereotypes most Americans have taken from inner city and poor Black youths and placed on the majority of Blacks.

To suggest that a biracial child should be raised Black is to say that the child must be pushed to excel to the potential that is peculiar to Black people both here in America and before here in America. He must understand that no White Privileges will go to him; everything that he gets will be worked for, and his work will be harder than his White counterpart (*Ain't no angel gonna greet him. . . . [Philadelphia—the movie's theme song]*); many of the things he rightly deserves will not come to him; he will face struggle—it is his *way of the world*; he *must* prepare himself in school to excel in life; he must persevere in this American life; he must understand that those Blacks who stand atop their fields are not there because anyone gave them a chance—they made their chances, and so must he; he must be made to understand that in spite of unjust weights against him, nothing is beyond his reach because he is from a line of those who have risen above those weights and other shackles that bind—it is a part of his long, Black history. This is the value that a biracial child must have, and his parents must give to him.

If a biracial child (Black/White/other) is not equipped with this worldview, he is crippled by *his loving parents*; it takes this stout worldview for a Black man in America to achieve to his potential. And potential is nothing unless it is achieved. And if this child fails to achieve, those who deplore mixed marriages or liaisons will tout the child's failure as evidence of the failure of these types of relations. And Blacks, on the other hand, may well accuse the White parent of being derelict in parenting the child because the child is a Black child. This is the rock and hard place the White parent has in parenting the biracial child!

No Love Without Discipline

The parent must become a guiding parent who forces, pushes, pulls, and demands his/her child to achieve in a *specific area*. You decide early on what his future profession will be and help him decide on it as a worthy future profession. Do not talk options; instill specific values from the time his understanding awakens. Options come after he has achieved the lofty goals and he is a man with a profession and brilliance worthy of his potential. We have no shortage of hairdressers, barbers, or basketball players—we always need more doctors, engineers, lawyers/judges, scientists, etc. Place him in courses that prepare him for these fields in college. Make him know that college is a given, not an option; he is not to even think about a life without a good college education; such a reality does not exist for him.

He can find himself later; he can have fun later, he can hang out with his friends later, and all the confused chatter and rationalizations of non-achievement coming from the non-achievers to justify their non-achievements should be summarily and absolutely discarded. No rationale for being less than his potential-realized should be allowed. *If he hates you for it now, that is the pain of parenting.* Once his eyes have become open, he will love you for it. But now, you cannot allow yourself to be as blind as he is. You are the parent, he is the child, your eyes are open, and you love him too much to allow temporal gratifications to harm his significant well-being. He must prepare himself now to take his place as he honors you and his total parentage and history. *Anything less than this in parenting demonstrates that you hate your child rather than love him. . . .*

A Black child, whether 100% Black or partially Black, has a rich and proud history from which to draw. There is a cloud of Black witnesses who have gone before him and who stand proudly today to lead the way for him.

Parents, it is not enough to give a child love, unless one understands what love is. Biracial children must be raised with special care because of the nature of this duplicitous society.

> *"While adoption does materially improve the lives of many individual children, at the same time, adoption burdens adoptees for life with enormous psychological challenges and emotional hurdles that must be continually renegotiated at different stages of the life span."*

Transracial Adoption Is Both a Blessing and a Curse for Adoptees

John Raible

John Raible is a biracial adult adoptee, the adoptive parent of children of color, and an assistant professor of diversity and curriculum studies at the University of Nebraska-Lincoln. In the following viewpoint, he argues that transracial adoption both improves the lives of adoptees and creates lifelong trauma for those adoptees. Raible explains that racism remains a serious problem in our society and notes that the adoption system is fundamen-

tally flawed. He concludes, however, that transracial adoptions should not be halted. Instead, he says, hard work must be done to reform both society and adoption.

As you read, consider the following questions:

1. What does Raible say worries him about changes in attitudes toward racism since the 1960s?

2. According to Raible, how does transracial adoption compare to transnational adoption?

3. Why does Raible say that transracial adoption remains controversial?

If this is your first encounter with my personal perspective on the transracial adoption experiment, I'm afraid that you are in for a bit of a shock. As a biracial adult adoptee and the adoptive parent of children of color, my perspective is grounded in certain assumptions that I have come to accept about our imperfect society. I use the tools from my professional field, multicultural education, to analyze and understand the dynamics at play in our society. I should point out that, while my perspective might at first come across as angry, cynical, or despairing, I remain fundamentally optimistic about our capacity to change ourselves as individuals and to transform society at the macro level.

Basic Assumptions About Transracial Adoption

To soften the blow, I thought I'd outline some basic assumptions I make that inform the work I do in the transracial adoption community. If you can agree that my assumptions have merit, you will find it much easier to follow the development of my thinking on transracial adoption and, more importantly, you will understand why I take the strong positions I do on the responsibilities facing families that choose to become involved with transracial adoption.

I am professionally a multicultural educator. My work is best understood as the use of education in a continuing quest to nurture, encourage, and support the development of conscientious allies in the ongoing struggle for social justice. I understand that my freedom is inextricably tied to your freedom, whatever your social identities and background happen to be. I truly believe that we are in this racial fix together, and that we need to support each other in figuring out a viable way through the irrational system of racialism that we have inherited. I also believe in peace and nonviolence, and that there can be no peace until there is justice. As a result, I understand the work I do as one person's humble efforts towards peacemaking, that is, promoting harmony through understanding, intentional action, and solidarity with the oppressed.

Assumption #1: *Racism is alive and well.* If this very basic assumption comes as a surprise, you have a lot of catching up to do! I think our society has come a long way in terms of improving race relations, but we still have a long way to go. As a child of the 1960s, it worries me that our collective sense of idealism that championed the dignity and rights of the poor and the marginalized and that stood for racial harmony, peace, and social justice have largely been abandoned, perhaps written off as positions that sound utopian or overly "liberal." But just because we are no longer as publicly idealistic as we once were does not mean that we have overcome racism.

Assumption #2: *Through no fault of our own, but simply by participating in this society, each of us becomes culpable for racism.* Some of us receive benefits from institutional racism, while others of us are denied access to society's privileges and rewards based on the color of our skin. As Malcolm X used to say, we can either become part of the solution or remain as part of the problem. There is no neutrality in the struggle to transform racism. The tasks before us that have to do with fighting racism require a moral and political commitment of our time, attention, and energy. Wishing that things would get better doesn't make them so. Hard work and dedicated, intentional action and reflection will help usher in the kind of harmonious anti-racist society we desire for ourselves and for our children.

Assumption #3: From the perspective of the majority of adult adoptees I have talked to, *transracial adoption and transnational (or international) adoption are fundamentally the same experience.* This is particularly true when parents and children do not physically and racially "match." Issues such as race, culture, identity, and belonging are pertinent throughout various types of adoption when parents adopt children from vastly different backgrounds. I have encountered enough international adoptees to understand the numerous commonalities between our experiences, whether we were adopted domestically from foster care or joined our adoptive families through international adoption. Parents who think they can sidestep thorny racial issues by adopting from overseas are fooling only themselves.

Adoption Helps and Hurts Adoptees

Assumption #4: *While adoption does materially improve the lives of many individual children, at the same time, adoption burdens adoptees for life with enormous psychological challenges and emotional hurdles that must be continually renegotiated at different stages of the life span.* As a paradox, then, adoption itself is both a blessing and a curse. As I've written elsewhere, I am grateful that I was adopted, yet I regret that I had to be in the first place. Not a day goes by when I am not keenly aware of my second-class status as an adoptee.

Assumption #5: *The systems that create adoption are fundamentally flawed and thus, continue to cause harm to families and individuals.* This doesn't mean that I think all adoptions should stop. On the contrary, I have devoted my adult life to helping social workers, parents, adoptees, and others figure out how to reform the practice of adoption so that more chil-

Growing Up in "Whitesville"

Q: I frequently hear you reference the fact that you grew up in a place you call "Whitesville." What was so bad about Whitesville? Why do you even call it that?...

To speak of Whitesville is to remind people, especially adoptive parents, that they have CHOICES. The problem of living in Whitesville, as I see it and as I experienced it in childhood, is that it can lead easily to ethnocentrism, to a false sense of superiority, as if the way that white people live is the best and only way to live. Whiteness then becomes the norm against which all other cultures are judged. Whiteness becomes the preferred race, the better race. Whiteness defines safety, health, security, education, civilization, culture.

As a child of color who was reminded constantly that I was not white, how do you suppose that made me feel? Everywhere you look, all you see is white people. I hate to be the one to point this out, but that's not normal. There's actually something UN-natural about that, given the way the world looks. Meaning that given that one out of four humans on the planet is Chinese—and that the vast majority of people worldwide have skin the color of mine, perhaps a shade or two lighter or darker—it doesn't make sense to allow children to grow up thinking that whiteness is the norm, let alone the better race. That is, if we are truly educating the next generation to become global citizens and to share the planet's resources equitably and responsibly.

John Raible,
"Growing Up in Whitesville: Mock Interview, Part 2,"
John Raible Online. http://johnraible.wordpress.com.

dren can find security and happiness in strong, knowledge-able, and better supported and supportive families. Reforming adoption implies strengthening ties between families, including birth families, adoptive families, foster families, and chosen families.

Social Justice and Lasting Peace

Assumption #6: *Transracial adoption remains controversial because it rests on contested ideas about race and family.* Transracial adoption calls into question the following: Who belongs together? How are groups recognized? Should various groups remain separate? On what terms might they come together, or rather, on WHOSE terms? What constitutes a family? Should "race-mixing" be encouraged or discouraged? If adoption is a service to children (and not to parents), why do we still allow money to change hands (between adults) when it comes to finding homes for children? When these kinds of questions go unaddressed and remain unexamined, the needs of one small elite group of wealthy individuals are allowed to override the needs of other larger groups with far less power and privilege. In my opinion, this dynamic fuels contention and ill will, and thus transracial adoption remains controversial. Even though they are hard to talk about, it is imperative that we figure out how to have open, honest conversations about race and about adoption.

If you've read this far and are still with me, I think you will find the rest of my work useful and my perspective informative. Remember, the ultimate goal for me is achieving lasting peace, which, in my view, can best be achieved through the quest for social justice and right relations.

Transracial adoption is an incredible privilege and an awesome responsibility. In the words of Tatanka Yotanka (also known as Chief Sitting Bull), "*Let us put our minds together and see what life we shall make for our children.*"

Periodical and Internet Sources Bibliography

The following articles have been selected to supplement the diverse views presented in this chapter.

Angie Chuang	"Haiti's 'Orphans' and the Transracial Adoption Dilemma," The Root, February 9, 2010. www.theroot.com.
Ta-Nehisi Coates	"The Black Damsel in Dating Distress," *The Atlantic*, March 5, 2010. www.theatlantic.com.
Robin Lloyd	"Interracial Couples Invest More in Kids," LiveScience.com, October 25, 2007. www.livescience.com.
Latoya Peterson	"On Discussions of Transracial Adoption," Racialicious, February 1, 2010. www.racialicious.com.
Pew Research Center	"Almost All Millennials Accept Interracial Dating and Marriage," February 1, 2010. http://pewresearch.org.
Racialicious	"Interracial Dating: 'Beyond Race' Versus 'Anti-Racist Dating,'" August 13, 2008. www.racialicious.com.
Jessica Ravitz	"Transracial Adoptions: A 'Feel Good' Act or No 'Big Deal'?," CNN, May 6, 2010. http://articles.cnn.com.
Jill Scott	"Commentary: Jill Scott Talks Interracial Dating," *Essence*, March 26, 2010. www.essence.com.
Jay Spark	"The White Boy Speaks on Dating Asian Women," *Asiance Magazine*, November 7, 2007. www.asiancemagazine.com.

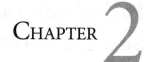

CHAPTER 2

What Impact Does Immigration Have on Interracial America?

Chapter Preface

A large illegal immigrant population exists in the United States. In 2007 the illegal population in the country reached 12.5 million. Since then a decline has occurred, but as of 2009, 10.8 million illegal immigrants remained in the country, according to Steven A. Camarota and Karen Jensenius in a 2009 article on the Center for Immigration Studies website.

How to reduce the number of illegal immigrants has been an exceedingly controversial issue in the United States. Federal and state governments have tried different, sometimes contradictory policies. One of the most contentious efforts to address illegal immigration was undertaken in Arizona in 2010.

In April of that year, Arizona passed a "law, which proponents and critics alike said was the broadest and strictest immigration measure in generations, would make the failure to carry immigration documents a crime and give the police broad power to detain anyone suspected of being in the country illegally," according to Randal Archibold in an April 23, 2010, article in the *New York Times*.

Opponents of the immigration law argued that it would encourage police to harass minority groups, especially Hispanics, without probable cause. For example, Conor Friedersdorf argued in a May 18, 2010, article in the *Atlantic* that the sheriff's department in Maricopa County, Arizona, had a history of abuses associated with immigration enforcement and was under investigation for profiling Latinos, avoiding oversight, and violating civil rights. Given that, Friedersdorf concluded, "The recent history of Maricopa County suggests that local enforcement of immigration law is bad policy, prone to serious abuses of civil liberties, imposes costs on taxpayers that far outweigh its benefits, and exact a high opportunity cost as officers focus on illegal immigrant laborers while more serious crimes go unpunished and 911 calls take significantly longer to answer."

Supporters of the law, however, argued that the federal government was not dealing with illegal immigration and that Arizona, a border state, therefore had to confront the problem for the good of its citizens. Writing in an April 28, 2010, op-ed in the *New York Times*, Kris W. Kobach stated that "Arizona is the ground zero of illegal immigration. Phoenix is the hub of human smuggling and the kidnapping capital of America, with more than 240 incidents reported in 2008." Given this, Kobach concluded, the new Arizona immigration law was a "measured, reasonable step to give Arizona police officers another tool" in handling illegal immigration.

In July of 2010 a federal district court blocked the most controversial provisions of the Arizona law, including those requiring police to check the immigration status of those arrested or stopped. The case continued to move through the courts as of early 2011. Meanwhile, other states, such as Pennsylvania, have considered passing laws similar to Arizona's.

The following viewpoints will consider other controversies surrounding immigration and race in America.

> "Taken as a whole, the research on His-
> panic assimilation presents two possible
> conclusions. Either Hispanic assimila-
> tion will be exceedingly slow ... or it
> will not happen."

Hispanic Immigrants Are an Unprecedented Danger to American Values

Jason Richwine

Jason Richwine is a senior policy analyst in the Heritage Foundation's Center for Data Analysis and a former National Research Initiative fellow at the American Enterprise Institute (AEI). In the following viewpoint, he argues that Hispanic im-migrants have been much slower to assimilate than earlier im-migrants from Southern and Eastern Europe. Specifically, he says Hispanics remain at lower income and educational levels for generations in comparison to white peers. Richwine warns that Hispanic failure to assimilate may damage the US economy and create cultural divisions. He suggests reducing the number of im-migrants who come into the United States and selecting more carefully for immigrants who will be economically successful.

As you read, consider the following questions:

1. According to Richwine, why is assimilation of Hispanic immigrants more important than assimilation of Slovenian immigrants?

2. Richwine says that second-generation Hispanic immigrants make up a great deal of economic ground. Why does he feel that this good news is not sufficient?

3. What does Richwine think the United States should learn from the immigration policies of Canada and Australia?

They're not just like the Irish—or the Italians or the Poles, for that matter. The large influx of Hispanic immigrants after 1965 represents a unique assimilation challenge for the United States. Many optimistic observers have assumed—incorrectly, it turns out—that Hispanic immigrants will follow the same economic trajectory European immigrants did in the early part of the last century. Many of those Europeans came to America with no money and few skills, but their status steadily improved. Their children outperformed them, and their children's children were often indistinguishable from the "founding stock." The speed of economic assimilation varied somewhat by ethnic group, but three generations were typically enough to turn "ethnics" into plain old Americans.

Hispanics Are Different

This would be the preferred outcome for the tens of millions of Hispanic Americans, who are significantly poorer and less educated on average than native whites. When immigration skeptics question the wisdom of importing so many unskilled people into our nation at one time, the most common response cites the remarkable progress of Europeans a century ago. "People used to say the Irish or the Poles would always be poor, but look at them today!" For Hispanics, we are led to believe, the same thing will happen.

But that claim isn't true. Though about three-quarters of Hispanics living in the U.S. today are either immigrants or the children of immigrants, a significant number have roots here going back many generations. We have several ways to measure their intergenerational progress, and the results leave little room for optimism about their prospects for assimilation.

Before detailing some of those analyses, we should recognize the importance of this question. If we were to discover that, say, Slovenian immigrants did not assimilate over several generations, there would be little cause for alarm. There are simply too few Slovenian Americans to change our society in a meaningful way. Hispanics, on the other hand, have risen from 4 percent to 15 percent of the American population since 1970. The Census Bureau projects that, if there is no change in immigration policy, 30 percent of the nation will be Hispanic by 2050. To avoid developing a large economic underclass, we need to confront the question of whether they will assimilate.

The children of Hispanic immigrants (the second generation) actually stay in school much longer and earn a considerably higher wage than their parents. In fact, the Hispanic rate of assimilation from the first to the second generation is only slightly lower than the assimilation rate of more successful groups of immigrants. Most second-generation Hispanics make up nearly as much ground as the children of European immigrants would if they grew up in the same disadvantaged situation.

But the good news ends there, and two problems arise. First, the second generation still does not come close to matching the socioeconomic status of white natives. Even if Hispanics were to keep climbing the ladder each generation, their assimilation would be markedly slower than that of other groups. But even that view is overly optimistic, because of the

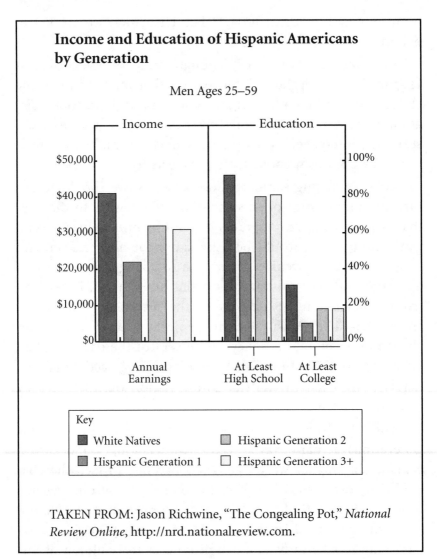

Income and Education of Hispanic Americans by Generation

Men Ages 25–59

TAKEN FROM: Jason Richwine, "The Congealing Pot," *National Review Online*, http://nrd.nationalreview.com.

second, larger problem with Hispanic assimilation: It appears to stall after the second generation. We see little further ladder-climbing from the grandchildren of Hispanic immigrants. They do not rise out of the lower class.

Earnings and Education Lag

The most straightforward statistical evidence of this stall in Hispanic assimilation comes from the Current Population

Survey (CPS), which asks respondents their ethnicity, where they were born, and where their parents were born. From this information we can construct an account of the first generation (foreign-born), the second generation (born in the U.S. with at least one foreign-born parent), and the "3+" generations (born in the U.S. to two U.S.-born parents) among the Hispanic respondents. . . .

The annual earnings of second-generation Hispanic men are substantially higher than those of the first generation. However, the 3+ generations have about the same earnings as the second, still well below white natives. No generational progress beyond the second generation is evident.

The educational picture does not look much better. The children of Hispanic immigrants are much better educated than their parents. However, American-born Hispanics still have high dropout and low college-completion rates compared with white natives, and there is little improvement from the second to the 3+ generations. Again, progress stalls.

These results do not depend on the time period considered. Economists Jeffrey Grogger and Stephen Trejo reached the same conclusions when they used CPS data from the mid-1990s for a similar analysis of Mexican Americans. And other datasets tell the same story. One study reported results from the Latino National Political Survey, conducted in 1989 and 1990. Among its striking findings was that the percentage of Mexican-American households with incomes higher than $50,000 rose from 7 percent in the first generation to 11 percent in the second. But the same statistic in the third and fourth generations stayed at 11 percent, at a time when the national rate was 24 percent. Another study, the National Longitudinal Survey of Youth, began tracking a representative sample of young Americans in 1979. By 1993, the Hispanic 3+ generations in that sample had, if anything, slightly *worse* outcomes than the second generation in terms of wages, educational attainment, and cognitive test scores.

The studies discussed so far are cross-sectional—statistical snapshots captured at single points in time. Since each of the generations being compared lives in the same era, the second-generation respondents are not the actual children of the first generation, nor are the third-generation respondents the children of the second. But longitudinal studies—taking one cohort of Hispanic immigrants, then examining their children and their children's children over several decades—tell a similarly pessimistic story.

Few Gains over Time

Economist James P. Smith pieced together census and CPS data starting in 1940 and ending in 1997. He was able to compare eight different immigrant birth cohorts with their children and grandchildren in later years. Smith found that, contrary to the cross-sectional studies, the Hispanic educational deficit relative to whites did become smaller between the second and 3+ generations. This might indicate an increase in their skills relative to whites, but it might also reflect the trend in the mid-20th century for working-class people to stay in school longer. Did the educational gains for Hispanics affect their relative earning power?

Not by much. The ... [data] from Smith's study, shows average Hispanic-American and Mexican-American earnings by birth cohort and generation as a percentage of average white-native earnings. In the six most recent cohorts, the Hispanic panel shows only modest gains from the second to the 3+ generations. For example, Hispanic immigrants born between 1915 and 1919 earned 70.9 percent of what contemporary white natives earned. The children of those immigrants earned 82.3 percent, and the immigrants' grandchildren earned 84.8 percent. For Mexicans in particular the picture is even worse. In five of the six most recent birth cohorts, the Mexican 3+ generations earn a marginally *lower* fraction of the white-native wage than does the second generation.

A similar longitudinal analysis was recently conducted by UCLA sociologists Edward E. Telles and Vilma Ortiz. They revived a 1960s-era cross-sectional survey of Mexican Americans by re-interviewing many of the original respondents more than 40 years later. By adding information about the parents and children of the respondents in this second survey wave, the authors were able to construct a longitudinal dataset similar to Smith's. Their results show continued improvement in high school–graduation rates from the second to the 3+ generations, but small gains in college graduation and stagnant relative wages.

Taken as a whole, the research on Hispanic assimilation presents two possible conclusions. Either Hispanic assimilation will be exceedingly slow—taking at least four or five generations, and probably several more—or it will not happen. In either case, Hispanic immigration will have a serious long-term consequence: The grandchildren of today's Hispanic immigrants will lag far behind the grandchildren of today's white natives.

No Easy Solutions

So why do Hispanics, on average, not assimilate? Theories abound. Popular explanations from the Left include the legacy of white racism, labor-market discrimination, housing segregation, and poor educational opportunities. Those on the Right tend to cite enforced multiculturalism, ethnic enclaves, and a self-perpetuating culture of poverty. One would need a whole book to sort out these competing explanations, but we can safely say that none of them, even if true, suggests easy solutions. Social scientists have not devised any set of programs that effectively spurs assimilation.

That assimilation has stalled even among third-generation Hispanics growing up today is especially sobering. In the early 20th century, the quality of schools varied greatly, high school graduation was unusual, travel was relatively difficult, and universities and employers were free to discriminate based on ethnicity. Today all but the worst inner-city schools are well funded, high school graduation is expected, traveling around the country to look for work is much easier, and affirmative-action programs give preferences to Hispanics. Despite these advantages over earlier immigrants, today's Hispanics have not closed the socioeconomic gap with white natives.

Though continuing research on the barriers to Hispanic assimilation will be valuable, the reality is that no intervention in the foreseeable future will change the very slow and perhaps nonexistent assimilation process into a fast and effective one.

The consequences of a large ethno-cultural group's lagging behind the majority in education and income are significant. In strictly economic terms, perpetually poor immigrants and their descendants will be a major strain on social spending and infrastructure. Health care, public education, welfare payments, the criminal justice system, and programs for affordable housing will all require more tax dollars. When pro-immigration conservatives declare that these government programs should be scaled back or eliminated entirely, I am sympathetic. But a large public sector is a reality that cannot be wished away—we will not be abolishing Medicaid or public schools anytime soon. Immigration policy needs to take that reality into account.

Even if economics were not a concern, the lack of Hispanic assimilation is likely to create ethnic tensions that threaten our cultural core. Human beings are a tribal species, and this makes ethnicity a natural fault line in any society. Intra-European ethnic divisions have been largely overcome through economic assimilation—Irish and Italian immigrants may have looked a bit different from natives, but by the third generation their socioeconomic profiles were similar. Hispanic Americans do not have that benefit.

Persistent ethnic disparities in socioeconomic status add to a sense of "otherness" felt by minorities outside the economic mainstream. Though it is encouraging that Hispanics often profess a belief in the American creed, an undercurrent of this "otherness" is still apparent. For example, a Pew Hispanic Center survey in 2002 asked American-born Hispanics "which terms they would use *first* to describe themselves." Less than half (46 percent) said "American," while the majority said they primarily identified either with their ancestral country or as simply Hispanic or Latino. This feeling of otherness probably helps spur explicit ethnic organizing and lobbying. Already there is a long list of Hispanic interest groups—the National Council of La Raza, the Congressional Hispanic Caucus Institute, the U.S. Hispanic Chamber of Commerce, the National Association of Hispanic Journalists, and the Hispanic Lobbyists Association, to name just a handful. If Hispanics fail to assimilate, these groups will remain powerful, and they will continue to encourage Hispanics and other Americans to view our society in terms of inter-ethnic competition. It is difficult to see how a unifying national culture can be preserved and extended in that environment.

Reduce Immigration

Two major changes to our immigration policy are needed to remedy the assimilation problem. First, we should drastically reduce illegal immigration. In the early part of this decade, the illegal-immigrant population saw a net increase of about 515,000 people per year, two-thirds of whom were from Mexico and Central America. The recession appears to have reduced illegal border crossings significantly, but the problem will surely return when our economy improves.

The second change concerns our *legal* immigration system. While it is important that spouses and minor children of U.S. citizens be allowed to immigrate, our present policy extends well beyond the nuclear family. U.S. citizens can sponsor their parents; their adult children, who may bring their own spouses and children with them; and their adult brothers and sisters, who may also bring their own spouses and children with them. These new green-card holders can then acquire citizenship and bring in their own extended families, perpetuating the cycle. This is "chain migration," and it causes the number of unskilled immigrants in the U.S. to increase swiftly.

It need not continue. Instead of bringing large extended families with limited skills into the U.S., we could specifically select for the qualities—education and work experience, for example—that help immigrants succeed. How would such a system work? We need only look north to see it in practice. Canada assigns points to potential immigrants for various desirable characteristics. For example, holding a graduate degree is worth five times as many points as is holding a high-school diploma. Australia has a similar system. In fact, Canada and Australia take in proportionally three to four times as many immigrants for economic reasons as the U.S. does, and fewer than half as many for family reunification.

Of course, precisely which factors to select for is itself a controversial question, and should be debated in the political arena. But that debate can begin only when we let go of our sepia-toned memories of immigration past. Who gets in really does matter, and we should not let the success of Europeans who came here a hundred years ago obscure that fact.

"The demagogic portrayal of Mexico as
a threat to American culture, society,
and security has not solved the problems associated with Mexico-U.S. migration; it has only made them worse."

Hispanic Immigration
Is Neither Unprecedented
nor a Danger

Douglas S. Massey

*Douglas S. Massey is a professor of sociology and public affairs
at Princeton University and the coauthor of* Crossing the Border: Research from the Mexican Migration Project. *In the following viewpoint, he argues that Mexican immigration is in line
with what would be expected between two friendly neighboring
countries. He also argues that most Mexican immigrants are not
especially poor, that they consume disproportionately few social
services, and that their cultural impact on the United States is
far less than the United States' cultural impact on Mexico. He
concludes that anti-immigration rhetoric is largely demagoguery
and is not helpful.*

As you read, consider the following questions:

1. How long has the rate of undocumented migration from Mexico been stable, according to Massey?

2. Massey says that the buildup of border enforcement has not prevented migration from Mexico but has instead actually increased the undocumented population in the United States. How has it done this, according to him?

3. According to Massey, why is Mexico not a threat to US security?

[M]exican American author] Richard Rodriguez is an essayist in the humanist tradition and thus comments on the cultural meaning of Mexican immigration and the symbolic importance of Mexicans in American society. As a student of culture myself, I concur with his emphasis on cultural meanings and symbols in the current debate. Indeed, as I pointed out in a recent article, "the Mexico-U.S. border is much more than a boundary between two nations. Over the years it has become a symbolic stage upon which the nation's insecurities and fears, hopes and dreams, are projected for public consumption" and that as a result, "American border policy has less to do with the underlying realities of Mexican immigration than with the nation's view of itself and its place in the world." (*Chronicle of Higher Education Review*, June 30, B11).

Not a Tidal Wave

Despite my appreciation for the cultural ramifications of Mexican immigration, I am a social scientist and ultimately believe that accurate understanding needs to be grounded in empirical reality. In 25 years of research on a variety of public policy issues, I have never seen so much misinformation as in the debate on Mexican immigration during 2006. Thanks to the media and political entrepreneurs, Mexican immigrants are routinely portrayed as a tidal wave of human beings fleeing an impoverished, disorganized nation who are desperate to settle in the United States, where they will overwhelm our culture, displace our language, mooch our social services, and undermine our national security.

This profile, however, bears no discernible relationship to the reality that I know as a social scientist. Since 1982 I have co-directed a large data-gathering effort known as the Mexican Migration Project. My collaborators and I have conducted representative surveys in communities all over Mexico and the United States, and over the years, we have surveyed 20,000 households and 120,000 individuals to gather detailed information from U.S. migrants about their experiences crossing the border, living in the United States, and returning to Mexico. My understanding of Mexican immigration rests on these data, and if anyone thinks I've got it all wrong, they are free to download the data, analyze it, and see for themselves.

Mexican immigration is not a tidal wave. The rate of undocumented migration has not increased in over two decades. Neither is Mexico a demographic time bomb; its fertility rate is only slightly above replacement. Although a variety of transborder population movements have increased, this is to be expected in a North American economy that is increasingly integrated under the terms of a mutually ratified trade agreement. Undocumented migration stems from the unwillingness of the United States to include labor within the broader framework governing trade and investment. Rates of migration between Mexico and the United States are entirely normal for two countries so closely integrated economically.

Mexico is not impoverished or disorganized. It is a dynamic, one trillion dollar economy and, along with Canada, our largest trading partner. Its per capita income is $10,000, which puts it at the upper tier of middle income countries, not far behind Russia's per capita income of $11,000. Compared with Russia, however, Mexico has a much better devel-

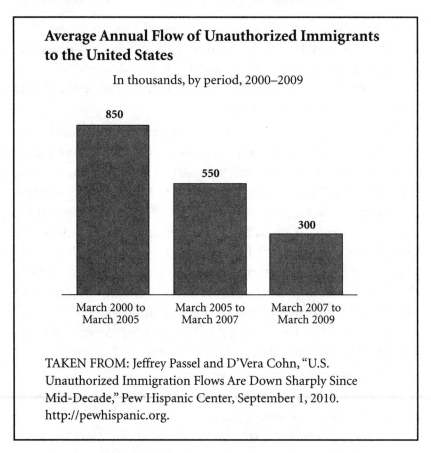

Average Annual Flow of Unauthorized Immigrants to the United States

In thousands, by period, 2000–2009

March 2000 to March 2005	March 2005 to March 2007	March 2007 to March 2009
850	550	300

TAKEN FROM: Jeffrey Passel and D'Vera Cohn, "U.S. Unauthorized Immigration Flows Are Down Sharply Since Mid-Decade," Pew Hispanic Center, September 1, 2010. http://pewhispanic.org.

oped infrastructure of highways, ports, railroads, telecommunications, and social services that gives it a poverty rate of 18% rather than 40%, as well as a male life expectancy of 73 years rather than 61 years (U.S. figures are 12% and 75 years, respectively). Unlike Russia, moreover, Mexico is a functioning democracy with open and competitive elections, a separation of powers, and a well-defined party system.

Cultural Influences Run Both Ways

In keeping with these realities, Mexicans are not desperate to settle north of the border. Most migrants are not fleeing poverty so much as seeking social mobility. They typically have a job and income in Mexico and are seeking to finance some economic goal at home—acquiring a home, purchasing land, capitalizing a business, investing in education, smoothing consumption. Left to themselves, the vast majority of migrants will return once they have met their economic goals. From 1965 to 1985, 85% of undocumented entries from Mexico were offset by departures and the net increase in the undocumented population was small. The buildup of enforcement resources at the border has not decreased the entry of migrants so much as discouraged their return home. Since the late 1980s the rate of undocumented out-migration has been halved. Undocumented population growth in the United States stems not from rising in-migration, but from falling out-migration.

To Americans who fear cultural displacement, I say look at what's happening south of the border. Cultural influences travel in both directions and in an integrated economy they are inevitable. Given the global hegemony of the United States, however, the cultural effects are asymmetric. We influence Mexican culture and society far more than they affect U.S. culture and society. Within Mexico, Wal-Mart, McDonald's, Toys "R" Us, and 7-11 are increasingly displacing Mexican outlets. Even Taco Bell is making inroads, and American cultural traditions such as Halloween and Santa Claus now compete with Mexican celebrations such as Day of the Dead and Three Kings Day.

Linguistically, English-speakers certainly have nothing to fear. English is increasingly spoken in Mexico and is viewed as essential for social and economic advancement. Even the smallest towns and cities in Mexico have bustling English language academies, and English has become a core part of the Spanish spoken by most Mexicans. Within the United States, in contrast, few Anglo-Americans speak Spanish and although it may be widely spoken among new immigrants, there is a rapid shift to English over time. Few children of immigrants use Spanish rather than English and virtually none of their grandchildren can speak it at all.

Do Not Build a Wall

Mexican immigrants do not migrate to take advantage of U.S. social services. Their service usage rates are well below those of other immigrant groups and have fallen sharply since the mid-1990s. Undocumented migrants, in particular, are more likely to pay taxes than to use public services, and even those they do use—mainly education and medical care—are consumed at rates well below what one would expect given their socioeconomic characteristics. The problem of paying for services to immigrants is serious, but one that is easily solved through federal transfers. Whereas tax revenues accrue disproportionately to the federal government, the costs of immigration are borne locally.

Mexico is not a threat to U.S. national security. It is an ally and friendly trading nation that annually spends less than 0.8% of GDP [gross domestic product] on its military. There are a million U.S. citizens living in Mexico and ten million Mexicans living in the United States, all of whom have multiple ties of kinship, friendship, and commerce that cross the border. Tourism is extensive and large shares of citizens in both countries have spent time on the other side of the border. Mexico has no resident Islamic community, no known terrorist cells, and has never been a launching pad for terrorist attacks on the United States. Those attributes describe our neighbor to the north, not our neighbor to the south.

The demagogic portrayal of Mexico as a threat to American culture, society, and security has not solved the problems associated with Mexico-U.S. migration; it has only made them worse. Rather than seeking to build a wall between our two countries, we should adopt the stance taken by the European Union when it integrated poor neighbors such as Spain and Portugal in the 1980s and Poland and Hungary today. Rather than seeking to block flows of people that naturally follow from trade and investment within a common market, we should work to make sure these movements occur under circumstances that are beneficial to all concerned, promoting growth in Mexico, minimizing costs to the United States, and protecting the rights of immigrant and native workers.

"Integration is crucially important to enabling American Muslims to fulfill their important role as a bridge between the U.S. and the Muslim world."

Muslim Immigrants to America Should Integrate and Assimilate

Souheil Ghannouchi

Souheil Ghannouchi is the executive director of the Muslim American Society, a charitable Islamic organization. In the following viewpoint, he argues that Islam's status as a universal religion makes Muslims able to integrate quickly and successfully into American society. He says that Islam enjoins its practitioners to be good, civically engaged citizens. He notes that US foreign policy and some anti-Islamic sentiment have been barriers to integration. But he says that Muslims will overcome such barriers through peaceful civic participation, voting, and lobbying.

As you read, consider the following questions:

1. What fraction of Muslims in the United States were born in America, according to Ghannouchi?

2. In what ways does Ghannouchi believe Islam's high moral standards will contribute to integration?

3. According to Ghannouchi, what is "the myth of return"?

The United States of America is a pluralistic society par excellence. It is a country that does not have a state religion, and Americans do not constitute one race or one ethnicity.

Immigrants have built the USA. Ever since Europeans began settling in what is now the United States by the 16th century, people from different parts of the world have migrated here. They have come from many different religious, ethnic, and racial backgrounds. Most immigrants came voluntarily; but some were . . . forced to come.

Moderate American Muslims

All groups have faced the challenge of preserving their identity through cultural practices, traditions or religious observances. Although many, initially, elected isolationism to preserve that cultural identity, they were later forced to deal with the challenges of integration into society and developing their new identity. The nature and magnitude of the challenges have been different for the different groups. The outcome of that process has spanned the whole spectrum, from total isolation to complete assimilation. Often, different segments or members of the same group/community have experienced different transitions through the different sectors of this wide-ranged spectrum. American Muslims are not different. Yet, only two-thirds of this Muslim population is from "immigrant" backgrounds—comprising four different generations of immigrants. The other third are mostly native-born African Americans, Hispanics and converts from other ethnic groups.

Muslims also spread throughout the different levels of this broad spectrum of integration into society. Conversely, the current trend is a rapid increase in the percentage of Muslims who were born and raised in this country. These American-

Muslims in the United States Are Assimilated

A comprehensive nationwide survey of Muslim Americans finds them to be largely assimilated, happy with their lives, and moderate with respect to many of the issues that have divided Muslims and Westerners around the world. Muslim Americans are a highly diverse population, one largely comprised of immigrants. Nonetheless, they are decidedly American in their outlook, values, and attitudes. Overwhelmingly, they believe that hard work pays off in this society. This belief is reflected in Muslim American income and education levels, which generally mirror those of the general public. . . .

Overall, Muslim Americans have a generally positive view of the larger society. Most say their communities are excellent or good places to live. As many Muslim Americans as members of the general public express satisfaction with the state of the nation. Moreover, 71% of Muslim Americans agree that most people who want to get ahead in the U.S. can make it if they are willing to work hard.

Pew Research Center, Muslim Americans:
Middle Class and Mostly Mainstream,
May 22, 2007. http://pewresearch.org.

born generations constitute more than two-thirds of those Muslims referred to as "immigrant" community. The vast majority of the remaining third, consciously, intentionally and willfully elect to be Americans by choice, choosing America to be their country. Most of these immigrants have lived in the U.S. for quite long times, and many have already attained citizenship.

The vast majority of American Muslims are predominately moderate in their views and attitudes. Their understanding and practice of Islam does not pose any hindrance to their integration into society. Accordingly, the two elements of their identity are perfectly compatible, so much so that they seamlessly intertwine naturally.

Furthermore, the median income and educational levels of American Muslims are above the average for other Americans. This imbues them with a deep sense of commitment to Society and societal stability. American Muslims have come a long way in integrating into society. They have developed a genuine and cohesive American Muslim identity as well as an integrative way of life. This process of integration promises to be easier and faster than other minorities. When compared with other minorities, Muslims have intrinsic advantages that can facilitate that process. The nature of Islam as a universal religion, coupled with the nature of a pluralistic Society of immigrants guided by a Constitution that guarantees freedom of religion and freedom of expression, make the development of an American Muslim identity easier and faster than for most other minorities.

However, this process of integration might slow down in the short-term due to Islamophobia and the climate of fear that has prevailed since the 9/11 tragedy [referring to the September 11, 2001, terrorist attacks on the United States], as well as the increased direct entanglement of the U.S. with the Muslim world. Yet, if American Muslims approach this situation wisely, they may well turn it into an opportunity to accelerate their integration. Such integration is crucially important in enabling American Muslims to fulfill their important role as a bridge between the U.S. and the Muslim world.

One Cohesive Identity

Being an American does not indicate anything about one's religion, race, ethnicity, culture, or views. Similarly, being a

Muslim does not indicate anything about one's race, ethnicity, culture, nationality or citizenship. Consequently, there is nothing that prevents the blending or fusion of these two components into one cohesive identity.

There is nothing in Islam that prevents a Muslim from being a good and loyal American citizen. Equally, there is nothing in the requirements for American citizenship that interferes with Muslim practices. It does not restrain them from promoting Islam or fulfilling their duty of encouraging that which is good and preventing that which is evil. Hence, the reference to the term Requirements is not limited to the legal requirements of citizenship, but also [extends] to the characteristics of a good and loyal citizen. Indeed, one neither needs to compromise any religious duties to be a good citizen, nor to breach any legal or civic duties to be a good Muslim. Actually, civic duties and Muslim religious duties blend harmoniously together. Not only does Islam mandate good citizenship, but also exemplary and active citizenship.

Throughout its history, the U.S. has accommodated all kinds of religions, ethnicities, cultures, and races. Islam and Muslims are no exception, especially since the vast majority of American Muslims are born and raised in America. They do not know any other country or culture except that of the USA.

As for the other Muslim immigrants, they have elected to be Americans by choice. They are grateful for the freedom and the greater opportunities they get in this country. All American Muslims have a stake in this country that they have chosen to be theirs, and in which their children and grandchildren will continue to live. Additionally, the religious obligations of practicing Muslims leave them no option but to work for the well-being of their country and to fulfill all their obligations and contracts that they have willfully undertook to honor when they took the Citizenship Oath, obtained Permanent Residency or filed a Visa Application.

The nature of the American Society and its Constitution facilitate the integration of any group into society, without forcing them to disavow elements of their original identity.

Indeed, in the America that accommodates all races and sectarian or racial religious groups, integration for Muslims should be easier, because they subscribe to and promote a universal religion. Islam is a religion that throughout its history has accommodated all races, cultures, ethnicities, and nationalities.

If it is possible for Japanese, Chinese, Indians, Jews, Africans, Hindus, Sikhs, and Buddhists to develop an American identity, it should be easier for Muslims to do likewise. Actually, this is absolutely possible because American Muslims include all of those ethnicities and more. Simply stated, Muslims do not constitute one race or nationality; and their religion is neither racial nor sectarian. Furthermore, not only is Islam, with its universal values, compatible with all cultures, but also its high moral standards do encourage the process of integration and contribution to society. Indeed, practicing Muslims restrain themselves from potentially harmful acts and behavior that may be legal, socially condoned or even socially acceptable norms (ex. drinking). Therefore, Muslims who follow Islam and might not be part of the solution, would surely not be part of a problem.

Muslims Must Be Civically Engaged

Just like everybody else, American Muslims can be any kind of citizens. However, practicing Muslims are expected to be, at the minimum, good citizens; and active Muslims are automatically active citizens. Indeed, fulfilling the mission of Islam requires active Muslims to be civically engaged, reaching out to people and maximizing their interaction with them. This will help to accelerate the development of a genuine and cohesive American Muslim identity. Consequently, to be effective in their mission of Dawa and Islah [enjoining good and forbidding evil], active Muslims must fully embrace that American Muslim identity. Indeed, The Qur'an teaches us that prophets were always sent from amongst their own people, using their familiar language to deliver their message effectively and efficiently.

It is important to recognize the main reasons that have delayed or hindered the process of developing an American Muslim identity that would have facilitated integration into society. The major reasons for that lapse are:

1. The "myth of return" which until recently caused the vast majority of immigrant Muslims to think of themselves as "temporary" immigrants that will one day pack and leave; therefore focusing on preserving their identity,

2. The sad reality that many Muslims do not adhere to the Islamic obligation of conveying and preaching Islam (dawa) as well as lack of activism, which necessitates and facilitates integration, the development and adoption of an American Muslim identity,

3. The misconceptions, among some Muslim groups, about the Islamic perspective on the necessity of positive relationship with non-Muslims and the fiqh (understanding) of citizenship,

4. The blatant and rampant injustices in American foreign policy, especially towards Muslim causes, and the American patronage of corrupt and oppressive regimes in the Muslim world,

5. The tragic experience of the African Americans, which has generated a great deal of resentment and lingering bitterness,

6. Most recently, Islamophobia, and the climate of fear that has been fueled by those who have used the tragic events of 9/11 to further their political or career goals.

The myth of return has, for all practical purposes, faded, and the vast majority of Muslims do accept the fact that they are not only here to stay, but are and should be an integral part of Society. Accordingly, MAS [the Muslim American Society] is tackling the other obstacles to integration by promoting the proper understanding of Islam, intensifying and diversifying Muslim outreach efforts and civic engagements. We believe that both bigotry and isolation tendencies are natural consequences of ignorance. Hence, it is our firm belief that education facilitates integration.

Work for Reform

As for unjust policies, whether domestic or foreign, past or present, our objections to such policies will not prevent us from being proud and loyal citizens of this country. On the contrary, it is the epitome of loyal citizenship to oppose injustices which is the responsibility of every good citizen and all observant Muslims. It is a virtue that is hailed by both Islam and the heritage of this country as well as protected by the Constitution.

Obviously, there are very many good and positive things in this country that should not be dismissed in resentment to those policies. Certainly, there are no countries in the world, even those with majority Muslim populations, that do not have some bad policies and laws. Ironically, in most Muslim countries, people do not enjoy the freedom of religion and expression, as they do here in the United States. Actually, many countries do not allow teaching or propagating Islamic knowledge, Dawa, which is normally enjoyed in this country. Paradoxically, such prohibition goes against the very important Islamic standpoint regarding the freedom to practice one's religion.

Most importantly, we have a system in the U.S. where the government is elected and can be petitioned, and that there is a reasonable level of accountability and respect for the will of the people. Therefore, all we need to do is to become involved and engaged, voice our opinions, advocate our positions on issues, and work to promote that which is good and reform or fix that which is wrong. In doing so, we are encouraged by the compatibility of the Constitution with our Islamic values.

Conversely, if we object to a policy, a law, a social norm, a public official, and/or even an amendment to the Constitution, we need to abide by that as long as it [is] in force, without relinquishing our efforts through civic engagement to change it if necessary. In our civic engagement, we will take principled positions that serve American interests, and express them in a relevant discourse to win over public opinion to those positions. We will join hands with those who share our positions. As for our opponents, on a particular issue, and our detractors, we will engage them civically and settle our differences in the court of public opinion, in the ballot box, and through legislation and even litigation—in other words, by legal and peaceful means.

> *"Rather than diminishing our differences and imposing integration, diversity should be embraced."*

America Is Strong Because of Diversity, Not Assimilation

The Sentinel

The Sentinel *is the official student newspaper of Kennesaw State University in Georgia. In the following viewpoint, an op-ed writer argues that the United States is defined not by assimilation but by cultural diversity. The United States, the writer says, has uniquely allowed immigrant communities and minorities to participate and succeed in society while still retaining their unique traditions and beliefs. The writer worries that with the Iraq conflict and anti-immigrant sentiment, the United States is moving away from an acceptance of diversity. The writer concludes that if the United States abandons its faith in diversity it will abandon its core values and betray itself.*

As you read, consider the following questions:

1. According to the writer, the United States is not like a melting pot but instead like what?

2. How did the writer's background affect his or her view of diversity in the United States?

3. According to the writer, how is the United States viewed abroad, and for what reasons?

What makes us American? Is it our common love for freedom, or is it McDonald's, *American Idol* and the War in Iraq? What defines us as a people or as a society? The truth is, America is a mosaic of numerous cultures, ethnicities, colors and religions—to the point where it has become nearly impossible to distinctly define the factors that make us American.

Home for Immigrants

From the time it was founded to today, America has been a home for immigrants from around the world. Ultimately, all of us in this country originated elsewhere. Once America took the initiative to open its doors to immigrants, cultural diversity became a great part of the country's identity. In the initial stages of the process, America was known as "The Great Melting Pot," a metaphor for a country in which people from all backgrounds combine and form a homogenous American identity.

The same cannot be said for America of the 21st century. The America I grew up in was nothing like a melting pot. It resembled a vibrant salad bowl—containing numerous contrasting ingredients which all came together to form one entity, yet each retained its own distinct flavor and identity. Despite having large communities of immigrants, American society does not necessarily compel one to abandon one's cultural identity and tradition in order to assimilate. Fortunately, the United States offers numerous opportunities and scopes to maintain one's own traditions while learning to cope and adjust with mainstream society.

My life itself is evidence of that statement. I was born in Bangladesh but grew up in the United States in a traditional Muslim household. I definitely experienced the challenges of growing up in two cultures that were complete contrasts to one another. Despite the obstacles, I never truly felt the compulsion to abandon my beliefs and value system in order to become a "True American" [whatever that may be].

Fortunately this nation offered me enough opportunities to pursue the American dream and still maintain my parents' traditions. By the age of four, I was able to speak Bengali, English and even Urdu with near fluency. I can honestly say that America's tradition of diversity was a blessing for me from a very early age. I still vividly remember my kindergarten days in New York, where school would begin with not only reciting the Pledge of Allegiance but also singing "My Country 'Tis of Thee," while my Sunday mornings would begin with reciting the Islamic Statement of Faith at the local mosque. In my early school years, the holidays were spent recognizing and even celebrating the Hindu holiday of Diwali, the African Kwanzaa, the Jewish Hanukkah and of course the Christian Christmas.

Truly, this was diverse America at its best.

America Is Growing Intolerant

Unfortunately, the America I grew to love, the nation whose diversity made me feel at home, is undergoing challenges towards the very trait which gave it a multicultural identity. With our increasingly intolerant nature of other cultures and ideas outside our nation—as we witness in the case of Iraq as well as our current immigration debates—we are in danger of losing the very identity which makes us American. Our policies abroad do not match the cultural tolerance we practice at home. Despite the fact that our nation is an amazing example of a vast array of backgrounds coexisting peacefully, nations abroad view us as ignorant and intolerant of other cultures due to the kinds of actions our government takes abroad.

The challenge stems not only from its behavior abroad but also in the alarming trends towards political correctness at home: imposing and dictating freedom to the Iraqis, coaxing other nations and peoples to adopt Western values and mindsets, fighting to close our borders and saying goodbye to immigrants who have already made America their home, doing away with celebrating Kwanzaa, Hanukkah, Christmas and pretty much anything that creates cultural difference. These trends all pose an intrinsic threat to the pluralism that makes America such a vibrant and thriving democracy.

Our society is a far cry from a melting pot. We have people from every imaginable background coming together to form an interesting and colorful puzzle. Rather than diminishing our differences and imposing integration, diversity should be embraced. Our differences should not be overlooked. In order to truly advance as a civilized society and so-called leaders of the free world, we should acknowledge and even encourage the differences among ourselves. Our questions regarding different cultural and religious traditions should not be pondered in doubt. Rather, they should be pondered with the intent of learning and understanding different customs and traditions. Cross-cultural communication and understanding is truly the bridge to building long lasting peace in our society.

This is not a bid for all of us to hold hands and sing "Kumbaya." It is a plea to make an effort to understand and appreciate the differences that make us who we are. Once again, I ask—what is it that makes us American? Our diversity. The willingness to accept, embrace and live with our differences makes us American. Our fine tradition of tolerance and acceptance of diversity in our society is something we can proudly define and claim as American.

If we are to retain our cultural identity [which holds acceptance of diversity at its core] we must continue our tradition of peacefully embracing cultural differences at home and abroad. We must practice abroad what we preach at home. Or else, in the fight to impose the American mind-set of freedom and tolerance to nations abroad, we may be at risk of losing this valued tradition in our very own home.

> *"With national unemployment hovering around 10 percent and black male unemployment at a staggering 17.6 percent, it seems even less likely that immigrants are filling only those jobs that Americans won't deign to do."*

Hispanic Immigration Causes African American Job Losses

Cord Jefferson

Cord Jefferson is a staff writer at the online magazine TheRoot .com. In the following viewpoint, he argues that illegal Latin American immigrants take jobs away from low-skilled US workers. Since blacks are disproportionately low skilled, they are disproportionately hurt by illegal immigration, he says. Jefferson argues that the racism of employers, who prefer Latino workers to black workers, also hurts African Americans. He concludes that the immigration debate needs to focus more on the effect of illegal immigration on black workers.

As you read, consider the following questions:

1. According to Jefferson, what evidence is there that in 2007 and 2008 Latino immigrants were more successful at finding jobs than blacks?

2. What are the six top occupational sectors for undocumented immigrants, and do these sectors employ black workers, according to Jefferson?

3. Why does Mark Krikorian say that immigrants are attractive to businesses?

In October 2008, amidst claims that one of its subsidiaries was knowingly hiring illegal immigrants, North Carolina poultry producer House of Raeford Farms initiated a systematic conversion of its workforce.

Competing for Jobs

Following a U.S. Immigration and Customs Enforcement raid that nabbed 300 undocumented workers at a Columbia Farms processing plant in Columbia, S.C., a spooked House of Raeford quietly began replacing immigrants with native-born labor at all of its plants. Less than a year later, House of Raeford's flagship production line in Raeford, N.C., had been transformed, going from more than 80 percent Latino to 70 percent African American, according to a report by the *Charlotte Observer.*

Under President George W. Bush [2000–2008], showy workplace raids like the one that befell Raeford were standard—if widely despised—fare. And though the [Barack] Obama administration has committed itself to dialing down the practice, Homeland Security Secretary Janet Napolitano has occasionally found herself the bearer of bad news to immigration activists who expected the raids to end entirely under her watch.

For the most part, the workplace crackdowns themselves are unremarkable—gaudy, *ad hoc* things that mitigate

America's immigration problem the way a water balloon might a forest fire. Increasingly however, their immediate after-maths—in which dozens of eager African American job applicants line up to fill vacancies—call into question a familiar refrain from the nation's more vocal immigration proponents: Illegal immigrants do work American citizens won't. Even former Mexican President Vicente Fox fell victim to the hype, infamously declaring in 2006 that Mexican immigrants perform the jobs that "not even blacks want to do."

Four years later, with national unemployment hovering around 10 percent and black male unemployment at a staggering 17.6 percent, it seems even less likely that immigrants are filling only those jobs that Americans won't deign to do. Just ask Delonta Spriggs, a 24-year-old black man profiled in a November *Washington Post* piece on joblessness, who pleaded, "Give me a chance to show that I can work. Just give me a chance."

Spriggs has a difficult road ahead. In this recessed United States, competition for all work is dog-eat-dog. But that holds especially true for low-skilled jobs, jobs for which high school dropouts (like Spriggs) and reformed criminals (also like Spriggs) must now vie against nearly 12 million illegal immigrants, 80 percent of whom are from Latin America. What's more, it seems that, in many cases, the immigrants are winning. From 2007 to 2008, though Latino immigrants reported significant job losses, black unemployment, the worst in the nation, remained 3.5 points higher.

Blacks Are Especially Affected

"I don't believe there are any jobs that Americans won't take, and that includes agricultural jobs," says Carol Swain, professor of law at Vanderbilt University and author of *Debating Immigration*. "[Illegal immigration] hurts low-skilled, low-wage workers of all races, but blacks are harmed the most because they're disproportionately low-skilled."

Immigrants Take Jobs from Teens

STEVEN CAMAROTA [director of research at the Center for Immigration studies]: . . . The study we're releasing today examines the issue of immigration and teen employment. I would say that there are lots of parts of this study, but there are three main things one should take away from this report. First and most important, the labor force participation and the employment rate of U.S.-born teens—that's kids 16 to 19—has declined dramatically over the last decade-and-a-half.

The second thing you should take away is this decline is a matter of concern. There is a decent body of research, and it's growing, showing that there are negative consequences for these kids down the road. If they don't work as teenagers, this can play out for the rest of their lives, or at least for a long time, as they move into full adulthood. And finally, the third takeaway point, or conclusion, if you will, is that immigration accounts for a significant share of this decline—that is, competition with immigrants for jobs.

"Panel Transcript: A Drought of Summer Jobs,"
Center for Immigration Studies, May 2010. www.cis.org.

Despite President Fox's assertion, of the Pew Hispanic Center's top six occupational sectors for undocumented immigrants (farming, maintenance, construction, food service, production and material moving), all six employed hundreds of thousands of blacks in 2008. That year, almost 15 percent of meat-processing workers were black, as were more than 18 percent of janitors. And although blacks on the whole aren't involved in agriculture at anywhere near the rates of illegal immigrants—a quarter of whom work in farming—about 14 percent of fruit and vegetable sorters are African American.

For their efforts, African Americans were paid a median household income of $32,000 in 2007. In the same year, the median household income for illegal immigrants was $37,000.

Audrey Singer is a senior fellow specializing in race and immigration at the Brookings Institution. She agrees that blacks are disproportionately hindered by illegal immigration, but says that pay is a necessary variable to note when talking about work Americans will and won't do. "There is evidence that shows people at the lower end of the skill spectrum are most affected by immigrant labor, particularly illegal immigrant labor," she says. "But would Americans do the jobs illegal workers do at the wages that they're paid? I don't think so."

Besides competing for work while simultaneously attempting to avoid drastically deflated paychecks and benefits, unemployed African American job seekers must also frequently combat racial discrimination. In a 2006 research paper called "Discrimination in Low-Wage Labor Markets," a team of Princeton sociologists discovered that, all else being equal, black applicants to low-wage jobs were 10 percent less likely than Latinos to receive positive responses from potential employers. Furthermore, employers were twice as likely to prefer white applicants to equally qualified blacks.

Racism

"To be blunt, a lot of employers would rather not deal with black American workers if they have the option of hiring a docile Hispanic immigrant instead," says Mark Krikorian, executive director of the Center for Immigration Studies. Krikorian's organization advocates a large-scale contraction of immigration to America, one of the main reasons being that low-skilled immigrants aren't contributing to the U.S. labor force in a way that American citizens can't. Nevertheless,

Krikorian says that easily exploitable immigrants remain attractive to businesses looking to eliminate hassles. "[Illegal immigrants] are not going to demand better wages, and they're not going to ask for time off," he adds. "And frankly, a lot of bosses are thinking, 'I don't want to deal with a young black male.'"

Most political analysts expect the debate over immigration reform to find new life in 2010, under a president who thoughtfully supports both increased border enforcement and the "recognition of immigrants' humanity." Wherever the discussion meanders, however—from amnesty on the Left to expulsion on the Right—from here on, it seems that anyone interested in speaking thoroughly on the matter can no longer do so without discussing its impact on black America.

This type of discussion has proved difficult in the past, however. "Many of the black scholars dance around this hard issue," says Swain. "They do their research in such a way that it doesn't address how immigration affects blacks. There's a lot of pressure to say the politically correct thing—that immigrants aren't hurting African Americans. Well, that's not true."

> "We will ask our congregants to see the immigrant as Christ does; and we will remind our communities that the true issue is not competition at the margins of society, but how society can expand opportunity for all of us."

African Americans and Hispanics Are United for Immigration Reform

Faith in Public Life

Faith in Public Life is a strategy center for the faith community. In the following viewpoint, members of the faith community including Luis Cortés Jr., the president of Esperanza, a network of Hispanic Christians, churches, and ministries, and Derrick Harkins, the senior pastor of the Nineteenth Street Baptist Church in Washington, D.C., argue that African Americans and Hispanics are not in competition. Instead, the authors say, they are united in a desire to promote justice and human dignity. They say Christian faith demands that immigrants be welcomed and their families respected. They also say immigration reform is necessary so immigrants are not persecuted, and all workers are paid fair wages.

As you read, consider the following questions:

1. Why do the authors say it may seem unusual for African American, Caribbean American, and Hispanic pastors to form an alliance to promote immigration reform?

2. What history do the authors say is important to remember in considering immigration reform?

3. According to the authors, what does valuing families mean in the immigration debate?

Dear Mr. President and Members of Congress,

It may seem unusual for African American, Caribbean American, and Hispanic pastors to forge an alliance for the advancement of comprehensive immigration reform legislation. Politicians, the media, and special-interest groups often reinforce the notion that our communities are at odds and in competition for jobs, public resources, and civil rights advancement. These same groups portray immigrants largely as Hispanics who flout the legal immigration system and deliberately displace American workers, damaging the opportunities and freedoms of African Americans. These images are a divisive tactic, used to prevent the possibility of true transformation in our system.

Justice and Human Rights

However, there is a reality that unifies us across ethnic lines and drives us to push for justice in this important human rights issue of our day. It is for this reason that Reverend Luis Cortés Jr. of Esperanza for America and Reverend Dr. Derrick Harkins, Senior Pastor of the Nineteenth Street Baptist Church in Washington, D.C., have convened clergy and faith leaders from across ethnic lines to form a coalition in support of comprehensive immigration reform. We know that blaming a particular group of people—rather than acknowledging and addressing the brokenness of our current immigration system—will never lead to real solutions for our nation. We also recognize that fear of those who are different will greatly hinder our nation's progress, and we must actively expose and uproot this element of the current debate.

We have not forgotten our history. Slavery was once upheld as God's way, until enough voices were raised to declare the truth about the injustice and cruelty of oppression. Slavery was followed by segregation, and now we are faced with the idea that the immigrant is a threat to our society—stealing jobs, bringing crime and even disease.

As leaders and men and women of faith, we see immigrants differently. We are called to care for the poor and welcome the stranger, and we stand on the principles of Dr. [Martin Luther] King [Jr.] and others who proclaim that God gave all people human dignity and value, regardless of race or position in life. This means keeping children and parents together, and establishing pathways by which our immigrant brethren may seek a better life for themselves and their families.

Compassion, Fairness, and Safety

We also believe that showing compassion to the immigrant does not require abandoning fairness and safety. We understand the need for our country to control its borders, and we see the need for real enforcement at the workplace, to protect against unscrupulous employers who lower the bar for all workers by subjecting immigrants to substandard working conditions and unsustainable wages. We also understand that the 12 million undocumented immigrants who are already living in this country must be honestly addressed, by ensuring that they register with the government, pay taxes and learn English. Finally, we understand that valuing families means we must not tear spouses apart or parents away from their children based on their citizenship status.

For all these issues, comprehensive immigration reform is the solution. It is both practical and just; and it reflects the direction and goals we should desire for our nation. Most importantly, it will begin to liberate us from the divisions we currently face, so we can turn our attention to the real challenge: how to build an economy and society that integrates and rewards anyone who wants to make a positive contribution to our nation's welfare.

So today, we pledge to take the lead in bringing diverse ethnic groups together to support comprehensive immigration reform. We will dispel the myths that allow our fears to be exploited. We will ask our congregants to see the immigrant as Christ does; and we will remind our communities that the true issue is not competition at the margins of society, but how society can expand opportunity for all of us. It is our responsibility to hold our nation's leaders to this higher calling. We pray that President [Barack] Obama and Congress will do all in their power to bring about comprehensive immigration reform. We pray that our continued efforts in our churches, our communities, and in Washington, will help supply them with the will to do what is right for all people who call this country home.

Periodical and Internet Sources Bibliography

The following articles have been selected to supplement the diverse views presented in this chapter.

Oscar Avila	"Blacks Split on Support for Illegal Immigrants," *Chicago Tribune*, April 23, 2006. www.chicagotribune.com.
Radley Balko	"The American Muslim Success Story," *Reason*, August 17, 2010. http://reason.com.
Steven A. Camarota	"Immigration and the U.S. Economy," Center for Immigration Studies, September 2010. www.cis.org.
Ross Douthat	"On Assimilationists and Nativists," *New York Times*, August 17, 2010. http://douthat.blogs.nytimes.com.
Conor Friedersdorf	"Europe, America, and Muslim Assimilation," *The Daily Dish* (blog), *The Atlantic*, August 20, 2010. www.theatlantic.com.
Steven Malanga	"The Rainbow Coalition Evaporates," *City Journal*, vol. 18, no.1, Winter 2008. www.city-journal.org.
Jay Nordlinger	"Bassackwards," *National Review Online*. http://nrd.nationalreview.com.
Stanley Renshon	"Why Not a Hispanic-American Identity?," Center for Immigration Studies, January 21, 2011. www.cis.org.
Reuters	"A Comeback for the American Melting Pot?," June 18, 2010. http://blogs.reuters.com.
Will Sullivan	"Hispanic Assimilation," *Hispanic News*, April 16, 2007. www.hispanic7.com.

What Policies Promote Opportunities for People of All Races?

Chapter Preface

The United States allowed the enslavement of black people for hundreds of years up until the conclusion of the Civil War in 1865. Even after the slaves were freed, African Americans continued to face legal discrimination and segregation until the victories of the civil rights movement in the 1960s. Because of this history of injustice and abuse, some advocates have argued that black Americans should be financially compensated by culpable governments and institutions.

In a May 5, 2010, article on his website, writer and educator Tim Wise argued that blacks had a strong moral case for reparations. He said, "The claim for reparations is not merely rooted in assigning blame for an injustice. It is rooted in the belief . . . that enslavement of African peoples led to the unjust *enrichment* of the West. The United States was *built* by the labor of the enslaved. White society was subsidized by the system of white supremacy and the economic base of the nation grew as a result of both enslavement and labor discrimination after the abolition of the same." Thus, for Wise, African Americans are owed reparations because the United States was built upon their unpaid labor.

In contrast, many commentators have argued that reparations are impractical and unjust. For example, President Barack Obama has spoken out against reparations, arguing that the best way to help African Americans is with programs that help all Americans. Quoted in an August 3, 2008, *Boston Globe* article by Christopher Wills, Obama said: "If we have a program, for example, of universal healthcare, that will disproportionately affect people of color because they're disproportionately uninsured . . . if we've got an agenda that says every child in America should get—should be able to go to college, regardless of income, that will disproportionately affect people of color because it's oftentimes our children who can't afford to go to college."

Tim Wise argued that "literally *no one* in the dominant political culture had been raising the issue of actually paying reparations." This is perhaps an exaggeration; in the Chicago mayoral race of 2011, for example, six candidates (including the eventual winner, Rahm Emanuel) stated their support for reparations in a debate, according to a February 10, 2011, *Sun-Times* article by Abdon M. Pallasch. However, Wise is correct that the concept of reparations has little political traction. Chicago politicians, who are in no position to pay federal reparations, can safely advocate them—national politicians, like Barack Obama, tend not to. Still, the debate about reparations continues, and may at some point move into the mainstream of public discussion.

The following viewpoints examine controversies surrounding other policies that have attempted to promote racial equality or justice.

> *"Professor [Richard] Sander testified that the primary cause for the black law school disaster is racial preferences."*

Affirmative Action in Law School Admissions Hurts Minorities

Peter Kirsanow

Peter Kirsanow is a member of the National Labor Relations Board and the US Commission on Civil Rights. In the following viewpoint, he argues that racial preferences hurt black law students. He says that black students are on average less qualified than white students for law school. Because of the small pool of highly qualified black applicants, racial preferences, he says, end up forcing law schools to accept under-qualified applicants. The result, he argues, is that many black law students attend schools that are too difficult for them. As a result, they perform poorly or do not graduate.

As you read, consider the following questions:

1. According to Kirsanow, what fraction of blacks entering law school will graduate?

2. Based on data from the National Assessment of Educational Progress, how do blacks compare to whites in reading, math, and science?

3. Under what circumstances did the Supreme Court case *Grutter v. Bollinger* sanction the use of race in admissions?

Startling testimony at a recent U.S. Commission on Civil Rights hearing from Dr. Richard Sander, professor of law at UCLA [University of California, Los Angeles], showed that racial preferences at American law schools are just such a sham. Professor Sander's two most recent analyses reveal extraordinary disparities between black law students and their white comparatives: The grade point averages of approximately 50 percent of black law students cluster in the bottom ten percent of the class. Blacks are two and a half times more likely than whites not to graduate. Blacks are four times more likely to fail the bar exam on the first try and six times more likely never to pass the exam despite multiple attempts.

A Black Law School Disaster

Perhaps the most astonishing statistic is that only about a third of blacks entering law school this fall [2006] will graduate and pass the bar exam on the first try. Bleak are the prospects for many black law students.

Professor Sander testified that the primary cause for the black law school disaster is racial preferences. His systemic analyses describe in unapologetic detail how affirmative action creates a mismatch effect, i.e., black students enroll at schools at which they're ill-equipped to compete.

Consider the progression resulting in the above failure rates. As my colleague Abigail Thernstrom has noted, the National Assessment of Educational Progress, "the nation's report card," shows that only 25% of black 17-year-olds read as well as the average white 17-year-old. Nearly 90% of black 17-year-

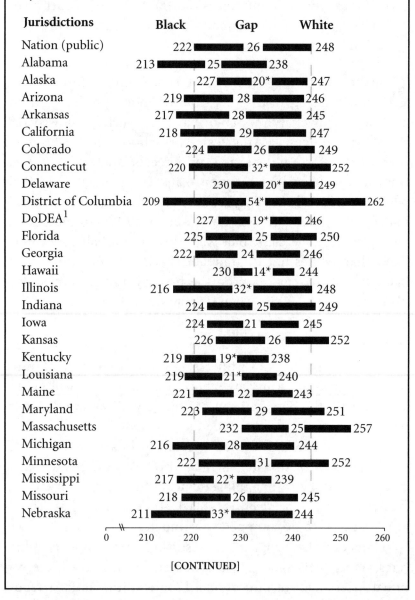

The Black-White Achievement Score Gap in Mathematics for Public School Students at Grade 4, by State of Jurisdiction: 2007

Jurisdictions	Black	Gap	White
Nation (public)	222	26	248
Alabama	213	25	238
Alaska	227	20*	247
Arizona	219	28	246
Arkansas	217	28	245
California	218	29	247
Colorado	224	26	249
Connecticut	220	32*	252
Delaware	230	20*	249
District of Columbia	209	54*	262
DoDEA[1]	227	19*	246
Florida	225	25	250
Georgia	222	24	246
Hawaii	230	14*	244
Illinois	216	32*	248
Indiana	224	25	249
Iowa	224	21	245
Kansas	226	26	252
Kentucky	219	19*	238
Louisiana	219	21*	240
Maine	221	22	243
Maryland	223	29	251
Massachusetts	232	25	257
Michigan	216	28	244
Minnesota	222	31	252
Mississippi	217	22*	239
Missouri	218	26	245
Nebraska	211	33*	244

0   210   220   230   240   250   260

[CONTINUED]

olds score below the average white 17-year-old in math. More than 90% of black 17-year-olds score below the average white

The Black-White Achievement Score Gap in Mathematics for Public School Students at Grade 4, by State of Jurisdiction: 2007

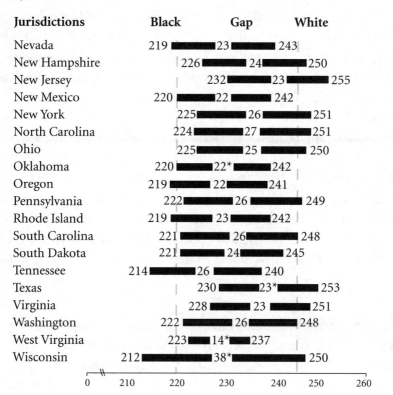

Jurisdictions	Black	Gap	White
Nevada	219	23	243
New Hampshire	226	24	250
New Jersey	232	23	255
New Mexico	220	22	242
New York	225	26	251
North Carolina	224	27	251
Ohio	225	25	250
Oklahoma	220	22*	242
Oregon	219	22	241
Pennsylvania	222	26	249
Rhode Island	219	23	242
South Carolina	221	26	248
South Dakota	221	24	245
Tennessee	214	26	240
Texas	230	23*	253
Virginia	228	23	251
Washington	222	26	248
West Virginia	223	14*	237
Wisconsin	212	38*	250

0   210   220   230   240   250   260

* Significantly different from the nation (public) when comparing one state to the nation at a time.
[1] Department of Defense Education Activity (overseas and domestic schools).
Note: States whose black student population size was insufficient for comparison are omitted. Reporting standards not met for Idaho, Montana, North Dakota, Utah, Vermont, and Wyoming.

TAKEN FROM: Alan Vanneman, Linda Hamilton, Janet Baldwin Anderson, and Taslima Rahman, *Achievement Gaps: How Black and White Students in Public Schools Perform in Mathematics and Reading on the National Assessment of Educational Progress*, July 2009. http://nces.ed.gov.

17-year-old in science. In the end, the average black high school graduate has the academic proficiency of the average white 8th grader. Accordingly, the number of black high school graduates ready to compete at the college level is small. The number who performed well enough to compete at elite colleges is smaller still.

Colleges must draw from this small, yet underperforming (relative to whites) group in order to satisfy their "diversity" programs. Admissions offices couldn't begin to fill their diversity requirements if black applicants were evaluated in the same manner as whites. A regression analysis conducted by Robert Lerner and Althea [K.] Nagai on behalf of the Center for Equal Opportunity shows that at some schools black applicants are more than 100 times more likely to be admitted than whites with the same GPAs and SATs.

Blacks flunk out of college at a much higher rate than whites. The black students who do graduate still lag far behind white students in academic competency—the gap that prevailed upon matriculation largely persists through graduation.

A Cascade Effect

It's from this small, underperforming pool that law schools in search of diversity must populate their classrooms with "meaningful numbers" of black students. The problem is that there aren't enough competitive black applicants to go around. As University of Texas law professor Lino Graglia pointed out a few years ago, the median GPA and LSAT percentile for admittees to the country's elite law schools were 3.8 and 98 respectively. At the time fewer than 20 black law students in the *entire country* met those standards. One elite law school, the University of Michigan, has about 30 black law students in each entering class. Michigan alone could snap up all of the black students at the median and still have ten seats left to fill. This means that in order to achieve "diversity," Michigan and the other first-tier law schools must dig well below the median to fill the remaining seats.

This creates what Professor Sander calls the "cascade effect." Using preferences, the top schools vacuum up all of the black applicants at the median, as well as those one or two strata below—leaving no black applicants who meet the unalloyed standards of the *second*-tier law schools. These schools must, in turn, employ powerful preferences to fill diversity seats with black applicants from the next level (or two) below, and so on. The result is that at most law schools black students are not nearly as competitive as their white classmates. Abysmal graduation and bar passage rates follow. And the pattern replicates itself in the job market.

The landmark Supreme Court case, *Grutter v. Bollinger* [2003] sanctions the use of race in admissions provided the preference is but a flexible "plus" factor—a feather on the scale—that's considered along with a host of other factors. But Professor Sander's research shows that the preferences employed by law schools generally don't comply with the *Grutter* standard. He maintains that on a 1,000-point scale the median gap between white and black law school applicants is 135 points. The preferences are overwhelming and, contra *Grutter*, applied mechanically.

One of Professor Sander's most interesting findings is that there's no credible evidence that blacks would underperform whites if schools used race-blind admissions policies. Blacks would then enroll at schools that are a more appropriate competitive match, thereby increasing the probability of graduation. He stresses that this isn't about race. Rather, other variables are at play.

If there was a product on the market that caused blacks, or any other group, to end up at the bottom of the class, flunk out in large numbers, and suffer in the job market there would be an uproar for the Federal Trade Commission to pull the product immediately, coupled with calls for congressional investigations. Lawsuits would abound. Not so with racial preferences. Maybe it's just easier to scam black students than fix the structural problems causing poor performance.

> "In a country founded on the notion
> that 'all men are created equal,' regard-
> less of parentage, ... legacy preference
> practices are fundamentally un-
> American."

Legacy Preferences in College Admissions Hurt Minorities

Laura Stampler

Laura Stampler has written for JewishJournal.com and as the Washington, DC, intern for the Nation. *In the following viewpoint, she reports on a panel opposing the use of legacy preferences in college admissions. Stampler notes that legacy preferences give preferential treatment to the children of alumni at many prestigious universities. The panel argued that these preferences amount to affirmative action for the wealthy while providing few real benefits to the university. Stampler concludes that the practice is unfair and un-American.*

As you read, consider the following questions:

1. According to Richard D. Kahlenberg, why were legacy preferences first instituted?

2. What is the relationship between alumni giving and legacy preferences, according to Chad Coffman?

3. On what grounds did Stephen Joel Trachtenberg defend legacy preferences?

With college applications at an all-time high and acceptance rates at elite American universities plunging, the gauntlet of college admissions has become all the more treacherous.

But what if the extra hours of test prep, perfected essays and community service projects count less than anticipated because many of those prized acceptance letters are already signed, sealed and spoken for based on criteria unrelated to achievement or diversity?

Affirmative Action for the Rich

While affirmative action has gone through the legislative wringer—subjected to significant public scrutiny and barely surviving a 5-4 Supreme Court ruling in *Grutter v. Bollinger* in 2003—the Century Foundation's new book *Affirmative Action for the Rich: Legacy Preferences in College Admissions* examines this less publicized but ethically precarious admissions booster.

The book is a collection of essays and articles by scholars, journalists and education experts arguing that much of what colleges have said over the years about alumni admissions preferences isn't true. A good summary can be found on *Inside Higher Ed*.

At a luncheon forum at the National Press Club in [Washington,] DC, on September 22 [2010], the book's editor Richard D. Kahlenberg and several contributing writers discussed the practice of legacy preferences in college admissions—which three-quarters of elite institutions employ—and which, Kahlenberg noted, were first instituted in the early part of the twentieth century to bar immigrants and Jews from top-tier universities.

Panelists cited studies conducted by Princeton's Thomas Espenshade, showing that legacy status adds the equivalent of 160 SAT points (on the old 1600-point SAT scale) to a candidate's test score.

Arguments for legacy preference often include assertions that the policy benefits the school's history of tradition and that it increases alumni giving. But panelist Chad Coffman's joint research analyzing the relationship between donations and legacy preferences in admissions, controlling for alumni wealth, suggests "no evidence that legacy preference policies themselves exert an influence on giving behavior." . . .

Fairness and Equality

In a country founded on the notion that "all men are created equal," regardless of parentage, said attorney and contributor Steve Shadowen, legacy preference practices are fundamentally un-American. Both Cambridge and Oxford universities have dropped the policy, he said. But what will it take to end the practice here in the US and how bad is legacy preferencing anyway?

Stephen Joel Trachtenberg, president emeritus and professor of public service at George Washington University, was the lone defender of the practice at the forum, stating in his opening remarks that the criticism "is all nonsense." "If [legacies] don't get into Harvard, they'll go to Yale," Trachtenberg said. "What we're doing here is rhetorical." Trachtenberg also cited a recent *Wall Street Journal* article which indicates that top corporate recruiters have turned a keen eye to big state schools such as Penn State, Texas A&M and the University of Illinois at Urbana-Champaign over Ivies [Ivy League schools] anyway.

Recruiters say graduates of top public universities are often among the most prepared and well-rounded academically, and companies have found they fit well into their corporate cultures and over time have the best track record in their firms.

Regardless of corporate hiring patterns, however, legacy preferences seem to clearly violate basic notions of fairness and equity. The bottom line, as Kahlenberg, an advocate for class-based as opposed to race-based affirmative action, observes, is that "with a legacy preference, we are advantaging the already advantaged."

> *"Education of bilingual students should be part of general school improvement efforts and should not depend on federal and state legislation. Better education for all students requires educational reform that includes bilingual students."*

Bilingual Education Is Necessary

María Estela Brisk

María Estela Brisk is a professor of education at the Lynch School of Education, Boston College. In the following viewpoint, she argues that the debates around bilingual education are politically motivated and misguided. She says that schools must provide a good education to all students. Part of that education, she says, includes bilingual educational resources for both English speakers and others. She says that bilingual education enriches classroom experience for all students.

As you read, consider the following questions:

1. Why does Brisk say the debate on bilingual education is wasteful, ironic, hypocritical, xenophobic, and regressive?

2. According to Brisk, why do national reform efforts avoid including bilingual education?

3. What is the first thing Brisk says educators need to do to achieve quality bilingual education for language minority students?

Much of the debate on bilingual education is wasteful, ironic, hypocritical, xenophobic, and regressive. It is wasteful because instead of directing attention to sound educational practices, it has led to advocating specific "models" based solely on what language should be used for what purpose. It is ironic because most attacks on bilingual education arise from an unfounded fear that English will be neglected in the United States, whereas, in fact, the rest of the world fears the opposite; the attraction of English and interest in American culture are seen by non-English-speaking nations as a threat to their own languages and cultures. It is hypocritical because most opponents of using languages other than English for instruction also want to promote foreign language requirements for high school graduation. It is xenophobic because it reflects negative attitudes toward groups of people seen as different. Finally, it is regressive because the rest of the world considers ability in at least two languages to be the mark of good education.

Providing Quality Education

The political struggle to defend the existence of bilingual education in schools has wasted much energy in the search for a "perfect" model and the best way to learn English. The recent history of bilingual education is replete with various models, all posing as panaceas. Overreliance on particular models often detracts from analysis of what actually happens in schools. When proponents of bilingual education let themselves be drawn into the battle over language choice, they too often lose sight of what should be their central goal: providing quality education to such students in ways that integrate them into both their own and the majority culture. If educators could ignore their particular biases about language use they would discover sufficient evidence to orient them toward providing effective education in any language. They would recognize that the mission of schools is to educate students so that they have choices when they graduate. Educating bilingual students has to go beyond merely teaching them English or merely maintaining their native language. The world of work demands that graduates achieve not only high-level literacy skills in English, and even knowledge of other languages, but also analytic ability and the ability to learn new things. Bilingual students have not only the potential but also the right to be prepared to meet the challenges of modern society.

Criticisms of bilingual education are not all unfounded. Some bilingual programs are unsuitable for delivering quality education even if they have graduated some successful students. Much of the credit goes to the heroic efforts of individual teachers. Advocates must admit that many bilingual programs are substandard. Rather than offering a blanket approval for programs on the basis of whether they use the children's native language, advocates of bilingual education need to be selective by supporting only those programs and schools that adhere to the principles of good education for bilingual students. Bilingual education too often falls victim to political, economic, and social forces that feed on unfavorable attitudes toward bilingual programs, teachers, students, their families, languages, and cultures. Such attitudes translate into school characteristics that limit quality education for language minority students. . . . Research on effective schools demonstrates that schools can stimulate academic achievement for students regardless of how situational factors influence them. [According to researchers Wayne P. Thomas and Virginia Collier,] "Schools with the highest achievement levels were so effective that the effect of these programs overcame the power of student background variables such as poverty. Low-income students were able to be high achievers." Considerations of language and culture facilitate English language development without sacrificing the native language and the ability to function in a cross-cultural world. . . .

Educational Equality in the Transformation of Schools

The rising sense of frustration with public education has called into question our ability to educate our students. The search for better ways to educate children has led to a proliferation of commissions, studies, and government initiatives . . . with recommendations to reform education in general.

> [According to researcher Jeannie Oakes,] In our quest for higher standards and superior academic performance we seem to have forgotten that schools cannot be excellent as long as there are groups of children who are not well served by them. In short, we cannot have educational excellence until we have educational equality.

One such population that has not been properly served is bilingual students: [According to researcher Alba N. Ambert,] "Language minority children tend to lag behind language majority children academically and the dropout rate for some linguistic minority groups is as high as 70%." The dropout rate continues to increase with new nationwide requirements to pass standardized tests in English for high school graduation. Some students are even encouraged by the schools to drop out and take the GED [General Educational Development test] instead.

Most national educational reform efforts avoid including bilingual education. Bilingual students and educators have been kept in the margins of education reform. There are several reasons for this oversight. First, various commissions' panels do not include experts in bilingual education; those that do, give them only a limited voice. Second, bilingual education is perceived as a politically controversial topic to be left up to legislation and court rulings to enforce implementation. Finally, it is seen as a compensatory program separate from mainstream education rather than a sound educational approach that can be integrated into the goal of foreign language development present in most proposals for educational improvement: [According to researchers Mark LaCelle-Peterson and Charlene Rivera,] "If the schools of the twenty-first century are truly going to be characterized by educational excellence for all students, they must be designed with all learners in mind—including those who bring linguistic *riches* with them to school." Despite research evidence on the value of quality bilingual education, testing requirements set forth by NCLB [No Child Left Behind, an education initiative] are undermining bilingual programs. Schools are succumbing to the pressure of testing in English by cutting down on the use of the heritage language for instruction, a cornerstone to good bilingual programs.

Education of bilingual students should be part of general school improvement efforts and should not depend on federal and state legislation. Better education for all students requires educational reform that includes bilingual students. Schools should be arenas where bilingualism is praised, cultural differences are sources of learning, and the main focus is on the quality of education. Schools where various languages and cultures are the norm with curriculum and classroom experiences enriched by this linguistic and cultural variety prepare students for the world of the 21st century. All students, not only bilinguals, need to find balance in their quest to become global, preserving their own individual identity as well. A cross-cultural school environment helps form such individuals.

Bilingual Programs Help All Students

The presence of bilingual personnel enriches staff resources. Bilingual teachers bring added knowledge and teaching and managing strategies that help increasingly multicultural schools. Such teachers contribute to the staff's understanding of bilingual students and to establishing ties with the communities of all students. They also provide added language models for schools promoting foreign-language education.

Bilingual and cross-cultural curricula support the goals of developing bilingual skills in all students. Second language development among English-speaking students is enhanced by a school context that values languages and promotes interaction between English speakers and speakers of other languages. Familiarity with culture not only supports second language learning but enriches factual knowledge and cognitive development. Claims that U.S. students do poorly in geography tests are symptomatic of their general lack of knowledge about the rest of the world. Incorporating in the school curricula aspects of the bilingual students' cultures will by extension improve American students' knowledge of the world in a very tangible manner. People of other cultures approach problem solving, personal interactions, and learning differently. Experiencing and discussing such differences expands American students' perspectives. At a time when technology facilitates contact with people of diverse linguistic and cultural backgrounds throughout the world, it should be obvious that schools need to prepare all students to communicate and relate in an increasingly interactive world.

Most successful bilingual programs have been created not by legislative mandates but by concerned educators and communities working together. Good education for bilingual students should not be the outcome of compliance with legislation. Schools must be willing to create good programs suitable for all students, including bilinguals. To overcome resistance to implementing bilingual education, many communities resort to politics or lawsuits to force school districts to provide bilingual education. However, political solutions create their own problems, paradoxically, compromise and rigidity. For example, laws and regulations that impose a 3-year maximum for students attending bilingual education programs arose as a compromise between the forces for and against bilingual education. Research shows time and again that students profit from long-term bilingual instruction, even though some students who stay shorter periods eventually succeed in mainstream education. [Researcher J.S.] Kleinfeld, in her study of an effective Catholic high school for Eskimo students, concluded that there was much that needed to be done to offer an appropriate education to bilingual students, but only private schools had the freedom to provide it. The present movement to forbid the use of languages other than English for instruction makes it practically impossible for families to choose bilingual education in public schools. Education is not about regulations, but about students.

Educational reform must consider education of bilingual students in order to include it in this country's educational improvement agenda. Advocates cannot accept any longer that the educational well-being of bilingual students is the pawn of linguistic and ideological power battles in Congress, legislatures, and courtrooms. . . .

Quality Bilingual Education

The question I set out to answer in this [viewpoint] is what educators need to do to achieve quality bilingual education for language minority students. First, they need to overcome many of the ideologically based practices that have isolated the education of bilingual students from the movement toward general educational improvement. By doing so, they can implement programs with the positive characteristics defined in research and experience, and promote meaningful assessment of students when programs are evaluated.

Advocates for bilingual students need to pursue their work on two fronts. The first front is the political struggle to support native languages in education, not just for the sake of language learning, but to provide comprehensible content education. More important, however, is improvement of the quality of education afforded to these students. The political struggle will avoid going back to earlier policies of imposing English at the expense of other languages. Research and implementation focused on what is actually happening in the schools will ensure that the bilingual programs deserve our support because they provide good education.

> *"Bilingual education is more expensive than other programs and is the least educationally effective."*

Bilingual Education Is Ineffective

Christine Rossell

Christine Rossell is a professor of political science at Boston University and the author of School Desegregation in the 21st Century, Bilingual Education in Massachusetts. *In the following viewpoint, she argues that bilingual education is the least effective and most expensive method of teaching students who are not proficient in English. She says that English Language Learners (ELL) learn the language more quickly when they are placed in special classrooms and taught entirely, or almost entirely, in English. She also says that ELL students should take the same statewide tests in English as other students.*

As you read, consider the following questions:

1. What statistics does Rossell provide to show that the number of students in Texas public schools who are not proficient in English continues to grow?

2. According to Rossell, how did former bilingual education teachers react when they switched to teaching sheltered English immersion?

3. Why does Rossell believe that universal testing of ELL students on state proficiency tests in English is possible in Texas?

Texas is a large, growing state due in part to high birth rates and individuals choosing to move to Texas from other states and countries. According to the state demographer, one rapidly expanding demographic is the Hispanic population, which is expected to double between 2000 and 2025 from 6.6 million people to more than 13.4 million people.

The Goal Should Be Learning English

The number of students in Texas public schools who are not proficient in English continues to grow. In the 2008–09 school year, Texas had 448,917 students in bilingual education. Between 1992 and 2006, Texas' English Language Learner [ELL] student population increased by 84 percent. Currently, 99 percent of the students enrolled in Texas' bilingual education programs are Hispanic.

As Texas' Hispanic population and immigrant population continue to grow, it is critically important that state leaders and policy makers look at the facts on how to best teach English to non-English-speaking children.

The goal of any type of program teaching English to non-English-speaking children should be learning English. Yet, opinions vary and tempers flare over which program—bilingual education or sheltered English immersion—teaches English most effectively.

Sometimes the term "bilingual education" is used loosely to refer to any type of English teaching program. For the purposes of this study, bilingual education is defined as instruction provided to students in their native tongue in all subjects in a self-contained classroom with other students that speak the same language. English is typically taught by the bilingual education teacher. English as a Second Language (ESL) instruction is defined as a program of small group English instruction by a certified ESL teacher whose students typically spend the rest of the day in a mainstream classroom. Sheltered English immersion is defined as instruction provided to students in English at a pace they can understand, taught by a trained ESL teacher, in a self-contained classroom with other students learning a second language.

Consider some key facts:

- Texas is one of only four states currently requiring bilingual education. The other three states are Illinois, New Jersey, and New York.

- Texas is one of only 10 states that have ever required bilingual education. The other nine states are California, Connecticut, Illinois, Indiana, Massachusetts, New Jersey, New York, Washington, and Wisconsin.

- Bilingual education is more expensive than other programs and is the least educationally effective. (Bilingual education is more expensive than mainstreaming or sheltered English immersion, and is less effective.)

- Students in bilingual education are not required to be tested on the English TAKS [Texas Assessment of Knowledge and Skills, the statewide tests] for the first three years. Testing all English Language Learners in English is the best way to hold schools accountable for the English language acquisition of their students and an excellent way to give schools credit for the extraordinary job they do of teaching English and content such as math and science to non-English-speaking students.

Trends in Student Population by Race/Ethnicity, Texas Public Schools, 1992–2007							
	Total	**Hispanic**	**Asian**	**White**	**Black**	**Nat. Am.**	**% Hispanic**	**% Non-White**
Change	1,035,162	875,900	73,117	-76,226	155,075	7,296	11%	13%
2006-07	4,576,933	2,118,867	149,817	1,631,680	660,785	15,784	46%	64%
2005-06	4,505,572	2,040,449	141,589	1,644,308	664,242	14,984	45%	64%
2004-05	4,383,871	1,961,549	133,010	1,653,008	621,999	14,305	45%	62%
2003-04	4,311,502	1,886,319	126,875	1,669,842	614,714	13,752	44%	61%
2002-03	4,239,911	1,811,882	122,229	1,686,534	606,141	13,125	43%	60%
2001-02	4,160,968	1,734,388	116,222	1,700,622	596,962	12,774	42%	59%
2000-01	4,071,433	1,650,560	108,605	1,713,436	586,712	12,120	41%	58%
1999-00	4,002,227	1,582,538	103,686	1,727,733	576,977	11,293	40%	57%
1998-99	3,954,434	1,526,713	100,143	1,746,896	568,757	11,925	39%	56%
1997-98	3,900,488	1,478,984	95,136	1,755,385	560,405	10,578	38%	55%
1996-97	3,837,096	1,435,521	91,051	1,750,930	549,667	9,927	37%	54%
1995-96	3,799,032	1,397,109	88,264	1,756,966	546,861	9,832	37%	54%
1994-95	3,730,544	1,347,613	84,933	1,750,213	538,742	9,043	36%	53%
1993-94	3,672,198	1,310,267	82,107	1,742,151	529,285	8,388	36%	53%
1992-93	3,541,771	1,242,967	76,700	1,707,906	505,710	8,488	35%	52%

TAKEN FROM: Christine Rossell, *Does Bilingual Education Work? The Case of Texas*, September 2009, p. 17. www.texaspolicy.com.

Recommendations:

- Adopt sheltered English immersion as the default for Texas public schools;

- Give parents choice to pick the program that best meets their child's needs in learning English; and

- Test all English Language Learner students on the English TAKS. . . .

Bilingual Education Is Least Effective

The data analyzed in this study suggest that bilingual education is the least effective program for ELL students if one's goal is achievement in English.

ELL students in bilingual education are tested in English on the TAKS at significantly lower rates than those students not in bilingual education. This indicates that bilingual education is less effective than all-English programs in teaching ELL students English and subject matter that they will have to know in English. The fact that Texas law allows such a discrepancy does not excuse it.

Trends in Student Population by ELL Status, Texas Public Schools, 1992–2007

	Total	ELL [English Language Learners]	Hispanic ELL	% of Hispanics who are ELL	% Non-Hispanics who are ELL
Change	1,035,162	332,527	309,319	2%	1%
2006-07	4,576,933	731,304	679,821	32%	2%
2005-06	4,505,572	711,237	661,768	32%	2%
2004-05	4,383,871	684,007	637,142	32%	2%
2003-04	4,311,502	660,308	615,281	33%	2%
2002-03	4,239,911	630,148	585,809	32%	2%
2001-02	4,160,968	601,448	558,694	32%	2%
2000-01	4,071,433	570,603	530,376	32%	2%
1999-00	4,002,227	555,470	516,601	33%	2%
1998-99	3,954,434	533,805	496,790	33%	2%
1997-98	3,900,488	519,921	483,320	33%	2%
1996-97	3,837,096	514,263	479,359	33%	1%
1995-96	3,799,032	479,576	447,174	32%	1%
1994-95	3,730,544	455,331	422,698	31%	1%
1993-94	3,672,198	426,059	396,437	30%	1%
1992-93	3,541,771	398,777	370,502	30%	1%

TAKEN FROM: Christine Rossell, *Does Bilingual Education Work? The Case of Texas,* September 2009, p. 17. www.texaspolicy.com.

The statistical analyses presented in this [viewpoint] demonstrate that it is the lowest-scoring students who are not tested in English. The correlation is clear: the lower the testing rate for ELL students, the higher the ELL achievement. The fact that Texas law allows local language proficiency committees to designate a Spanish rather than an English test, or exempt an insufficiently prepared ELL student altogether, does not invalidate a reality, namely, that both possibilities grow likelier if the student is in a bilingual education program rather than an alternative. When more weight is given to ELL TAKS English test scores in schools where ELL students have higher testing rates, bilingual education has a negative effect on achievement in English.

Finally, as noted in every other study of the question, bilingual education in Texas is more expensive than other programs for ELL students. That it is also the least educationally effective suggests that it is not the best program for Texas.

Recommendations

1) Adopt sheltered English immersion as the default assignment for ELL students.

Given that bilingual education is both more costly and less effective than other programs for ELL students, it is recommended that Texas follow the lead of other states and adopt sheltered English immersion as the default assignment for ELL students. At the very least, Texas should consider giving schools a choice as to the program that elementary ELL students receive, particularly in light of the fact that only three other states mandate bilingual education.

Research indicates that sheltered English immersion is the most successful program for ELL students *if* one's goal is the highest level of achievement in English that a child is capable of.... A sheltered English immersion course involves second language learners only, taught by a teacher trained in second language acquisition techniques. Instruction is almost entirely in the second language, but at a pace the child can understand. Sheltered English immersion is mandated as the default assignment for English Language Learners by Proposition 227, passed in June 1998 in California; by Proposition 203, passed in November 2000 in Arizona; and by Question 2, passed in November 2002 in Massachusetts. It is also implemented at the discretion of schools and districts throughout the United States.

My analyses and those of [researcher Valentina] Bali of the effectiveness of sheltered English immersion in California show a positive effect on reading and math achievement from dismantling bilingual education in a school. Through teacher and principal interviews in California in spring 1999 and fall

2001, strong support was revealed among teachers and principals for sheltered English immersion, even among those who had lobbied to stop the initiative from passing.

The former bilingual education teachers were now the sheltered English immersion teachers. The ones I talked to, loved it. In their previous experience as bilingual education teachers, they had worried about how much English their students were learning, but did not want to send their students to a mainstream classroom. Now these teachers felt they had the best of all possible worlds—a sheltered classroom in which they could use Spanish when needed to communicate with a parent or new child, but in which almost all of the instruction was in English.

2) Parents should be given choice.

Not every parent of an ELL child wants their child to be in a self-contained classroom consisting only of other ELL students, even if the language of instruction is English. In addition, parents who want their ELL child to be educated in two languages and understand the educational cost should have the right to request an alternative program, including a bilingual education program if demand squares with resources. However, the parent should have to come down to the school and talk to the staff about the programs for ELL students in order to understand exactly what they are and what the benefits and costs are.

One of the more shocking findings in years of talking to parents of ELL children assigned to bilingual education is that, despite being notified of the assignment, the parents had no idea of all its implications. They were unaware their child would be in a classroom in which instruction was at least partly in Spanish: almost completely so in the case of kindergartners. This confusion is undoubtedly a problem in Texas, where the default assignment is bilingual education. Although parents have the authority to opt out of a bilingual education program in Texas (as in every other state with mandated bilingual education), they are more prone to approve than to reject the default assignment made by the school, because they do not understand what their child is being assigned to and assume the educational experts know best. Thus, it is important to make the default assignment the program that is the most effective—sheltered English immersion—and not the one that is least effective—bilingual education. Then parents can become educated about the programs before they switch their child.

Testing Is Required

3) All ELL students must be tested on the English TAKS.

This is the most effective way to hold schools accountable for the English language acquisition of their ELL students. Interestingly, it is also an excellent way to give schools credit for the extraordinary job they do of teaching English and subject matter in English to non-English-speaking students. If a school or district tests ELL students only in English on the state proficiency tests many years after their arrival, they miss out on being given credit for the gains in English that ELL children made in the years before that.

Universal testing of ELL students on the state proficiency tests in English is required in California, so it *is* possible to do this. English language proficiency tests designed solely for ELL students—the Texas English Language Proficiency Assessment System (TELPAS)—are not a substitute for the state proficiency test, as one cannot compare the scores for, and the gains in, a test taken only by ELL students to the scores on a different test taken by non-ELL students.

The above recommendations are based on empirical research nationally and in Texas. Instruction in English (and the elimination of bilingual education) is overwhelmingly supported by the public, according to a number of national surveys and by voters in three states (California in 1998, Arizona in 2000, and Massachusetts in 2002).

A large majority of immigrant parents want their children taught in English, not their native tongue. Sheltered English immersion has already been adopted and accepted in California, Arizona, and Massachusetts—all states with large Spanish-speaking immigrant populations—as a more effective method of teaching English to English Language Learners. The Texas legislature should consider embracing sheltered English immersion as the default program in place of bilingual education.

Periodical and Internet Sources Bibliography

The following articles have been selected to supplement the diverse views presented in this chapter.

Ta-Nehisi Coates	"The Vanessa Williams Rule," *Atlantic*, May 18, 2010. www.theatlantic.com.
Amir Efrati	"Is Affirmative Action at Law School Actually Hurting Minorities?" *Law Blog, Wall Street Journal*, August 29, 2007. http://blogs.wsj.com.
Michael Franc	"Time to Set Aside Set-Asides?: With the Civil-Rights Race Won, Our Government Should Embrace Colorblindness," Heritage Foundation, January 28, 2009. www.heritage.org.
Bruce Fuller	"The Bilingual Debate: Transitional Classrooms," *New York Times*, September 28, 2008. www.nytimes.com.
George Leef	"Legacy Admissions—Affirmative Action for the Rich?" John William Pope Center, February 19, 2008. www.popecenter.org.
Jesse Rothstein and Albert H. Yoon	"Affirmative Action in Law School Admissions: What Do Racial Preferences Do?" *University of Chicago Law Review*, June 8, 2008. http://lawreview.uchicago.edu.
Tim Wise	"Affirmative Action for Dummies: Explaining the Difference Between Oppression and Opportunity," Tim Wise (website), October 22, 2010. www.timwise.org.
Mary Ann Zehr	"Bilingual Education Didn't Work," *Learning the Language* (blog), *Education Week*, September 14, 2008. http://blogs.edweek.org.

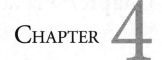

CHAPTER 4

Is America Becoming a Post-Racial Society?

Chapter Preface

Many commentators argued that the election of Barack Obama, a black man, as president of the United States in 2008, was an important step forward in race relations. Some used the term "post-racial" to suggest that America might be moving beyond the contentious issue of race.

However, Obama's presidential campaign itself had to deal with a number of serious racial issues. The most explosive of these was Obama's relationship with his pastor, Jeremiah Wright, of Trinity United Church of Christ in Chicago. Wright had been the pastor at Obama's marriage to his wife Michelle and at his children's baptisms. Wright is a "progressive minister who celebrated gay unions, ministered to people with AIDS, set up college scholarships and inspired three generations of a mostly black congregation that grew from 87 members when he arrived to 8,500 today," according to a March 19, 2008, article by Ken Dilanian in *USA Today*.

However, Wright also held very controversial views. In sermons, he accused the US government of creating and disseminating the AIDS virus. After the September 11, 2001, attacks on the United States, Wright explicitly blamed America, saying that "America's chickens are coming home to roost," as quoted in a March 13, 2008, ABC News article by Brian Ross and Rehab El-Buri. The same article noted that "Sen. Barack Obama's pastor says blacks should not sing 'God Bless America' but 'God damn America.'"

When Wright's sermons became widely known in March 2008, it created a firestorm around Obama's campaign. Many accused Wright, and by association Obama, of reverse racism and hatred of whites. Conservative radio host Rush Limbaugh, for example, in a March 13, 2008, broadcast stated, "This pastor, the Reverend Jeremiah Wright, he is a racist. He is a hater. Here is the question for you, Obama. Why did you join this church? Why did you stay with this church for 20 years? Why do you subject you, your wife, and your kids to this hatemonger in church as often as you go?"

In an effort to address the controversy, Obama delivered a speech on March 18, 2008, in which he explicitly discussed Wright and race in America. In the speech, he did not disown Wright. Rather he said, "I can no more disown him than I can disown the black community. I can no more disown him than I can my white grandmother—a woman who helped raise me, a woman who sacrificed again and again for me, a woman who loves me as much as she loves anything in this world, but a woman who once confessed her fear of black men who passed by her on the street, and who on more than one occasion has uttered racial or ethnic stereotypes that made me cringe."

Obama went on to argue that blacks like Wright have legitimate anger at historical injustice. But Obama argued that, "I have asserted a firm conviction—a conviction rooted in my faith in God and my faith in the American people—that working together we can move beyond some of our old racial wounds, and that in fact we have no choice if we are to continue on the path of a more perfect union." Obama argued that while many of Wright's grievances were legitimate, his anger and bitterness failed to take into account the racial progress America has made, or the racial progress America could make in the future. Obama concluded, "What we have already achieved gives us hope—the audacity to hope—for what we can and must achieve tomorrow."

The results of Obama's speech were mixed. A March 19, 2008, editorial in the New York Times said the speech showed an "honesty seldom heard in public life." In the following months, however, Jeremiah Wright appeared in numerous interviews and made more controversial statements, prompting Obama to permanently break with his pastor at the end of April.

Ultimately, the speech seems to have succeeded in its most direct goal. Obama won the Democratic nomination and the presidency. The Wright controversy, then, showed the extent to which race, along with the possibility of confronting it, remains an inflammable issue.

The following viewpoints examine other arguments surrounding the possibility of a post-racial America.

> *"Through such appeals to shared values,*
> *Obama is transcending any perceived*
> *racial or cultural gulf between himself*
> *and the overwhelming white electorate*
> *[in the 2008 Iowa caucus]."*

Barack Obama's Campaign Showed He Can Transcend Race

Scott Helman

Scott Helman is a political reporter for the Boston Globe *City &*
Region section. In the following viewpoint, he reports on African
American Barack Obama's success in connecting with white vot-
ers in Iowa as he ran for the Democratic presidential nomina-
tion in 2008. Helman notes that Obama needed to be successful
in the Iowa caucuses, the first state election for the Democratic
nomination, in order to demonstrate his ability to appeal to
white voters.

As you read, consider the following questions:

1. What does Helman say that Obama drew on to cast
   himself as a unifying force and appeal to Iowa voters?

2. What percentage of Iowans are white, according to the
   2000 census?

3. At the time the viewpoint was written, how much time
   had Obama spent in Iowa, according to Helman?

At first it seems like an unusual sight: Barack Obama, a black United States senator from the South Side of Chicago, trying to market himself [as a Democratic nominee for president] to white, rural farming communities like this one nestled between Des Moines and Omaha.

A Unifying Force

And yet there he was Thursday [August 2007], perched on a wooden platform in an open-air pavilion that smelled like livestock, seeking a common denominator with voters as they ate bratwurst, grilled corn, and watermelon.

"The basic idea is that we're all in it together—we rise and fall together," Obama told them. "People here understand that. That's part of the values that have been so important in Iowa and part of the values that are so important in Illinois. Those are the values we grew up on, especially in rural communities—you couldn't survive if people weren't looking out for one another."

Drawing on his white mother's Kansan heritage and his success in rural Illinois during his Senate race, Obama casts himself as a unifying force capable of seeing the country's woes from the vantage points of cornfields and ghettos alike.

Through such appeals to shared values, Obama is transcending any perceived racial or cultural gulf between himself and the overwhelmingly white electorate here, his supporters and Iowa voters say.

As a result, he moves easily through Iowa crowds in which he is often one of the few—and sometimes the only—African-American.

"Who's this sweetie pie?" Obama asked a man holding his daughter at the Iowa State Fair. "Daddy carrying you around all day?"

The Iowa Caucus

Obama's campaign is well aware of the message that a strong showing in the Iowa caucus [the first state election in the Democratic primary campaign] in January would send about America's white voters being willing to line up behind a black candidate.

"That's the big one," Terno Figueroa, Obama's national field director, told campaign volunteers at a training session last weekend in St. Louis.

Interviews with voters suggest he is making progress.

"A good, fair, honest man," said Roger Steffens, a 59-year-old from Atlantic who runs a bed and breakfast and has Republican leanings. "Race isn't important."

"That's one of the things I like about him—he can fit in anyplace," said Marie Mancuso, a 63-year-old from Ames, even though she is voting for someone else. (She won't say for whom.)

Some voters say they marvel at how Obama has been able to make such inroads in a state that is so white—94 percent, according to the 2000 census.

Iowa polls show him in a tight race with the other leading Democrats, Senator Hillary Clinton of New York and former North Carolina senator John Edwards.

"Yeah, yeah, yeah. We hardly have any blacks at all," said Robert Euken, a 79-year-old truck driver from Cumberland. "He [talks] about the wrongs that they're doing in Washington, D.C. If he can fix that, he's the man we want."

One weapon Obama uses in appealing to rural voters is his wife, Michelle, who comes from a middle-class black family on Chicago's South Side but is at ease in Iowa talking about their two daughters, and how she makes sure they are well grounded.

"The children in this country need to know they come first, and our girls do," she said in introducing her husband in Atlantic. "It's basic values."

Michelle Obama also touts her husband's crossover appeal by citing his experience in the 2004 Senate race. Obama won the Democratic primary overwhelmingly, capturing several rural downstate counties and white neighborhoods in the Chicago area.

Courtney Greene, an aide to Iowa governor Chet Culver, said she believes the acceptance of Obama is more a testament to the man than to the progress the country has made on racial harmony.

"I think it's both, but if I had to tip the scales one way, it would be to who he is," said Greene, who is black.

Spending Time in Iowa

Part of Obama's success connecting with Iowa voters also stems simply from the fact that he has been here a lot. Through last week, Obama has spent 35 days in Iowa over 20 visits, according to his campaign.

On Friday, Obama was in Tama, east of Des Moines, hosting a gathering on rural issues.

He met with farmers to gain input for his forthcoming plan to address the concerns of rural areas.

Obama said he would work to redirect federal subsidies from agribusiness to small farmers, make investments in alternative energy sources beyond corn-based ethanol, and bring high-speed Internet access to remote communities.

"I come from a farm state," he said. "I fought these battles for rural America. I've done it at the State House, I've done it in the Capitol of the United States, and I intend to do it in the White House as well."

Democratic Iowa Caucus Results, 2008

45 pledged delegates, 12 unpledged

Candidate	Vote*	%	Delegates
Barack Obama	940	37.6%	0
John Edwards	744	29.7	0
Hillary Rodham Clinton	737	29.5	0
Bill Richardson	53	2.1	0
Joseph R. Biden Jr.	23	0.9	0
Uncommitted	3	0.1	0
Christopher J. Dodd	1	0.0	0
Mike Gravel	0	0.0	0
Dennis J. Kucinich	0	0.0	0
Others	0	0.0	0

* The vote totals for the Iowa Democratic Party are State Delegate Equivalents, which represent the estimated number of state convention delegates that the candidates would have, based on the caucus results.

TAKEN FROM: "Iowa Caucus Results," *New York Times*, 2008. http://politics.nytimes.com.

Obama has written extensively on and sometimes talks about his mother, Ann Dunham, who grew up in Kansas, and his early confusion over his identity.

Alice Mullin, a 60-year-old from Atlantic who teaches at-risk high school students, questioned why people call Obama black.

"My response to 'he's black' is, he's half-white," she said.

Indeed, Obama's biracial background, nontraditional childhood, educational pedigree, and political history have prompted some black leaders to question whether he is "black enough," a question that has nagged at him since his days as an Illinois politician.

But here in Iowa, Obama's racial identity, at least for many Democrats, feels about as irrelevant as the color of his shirt.

"He's real sensitive to all the issues of minorities, and majorities, and everything," said Peter Wobeter, a 57-year-old farmer from Toledo, Iowa.

"He's just a real likable guy."

"The idea that Obama was ever really about transcending race flies completely in the face of his own writings."

Barack Obama's Campaign Did Not Transcend Race

Jonah Goldberg

Jonah Goldberg is editor at large of National Review Online *and a columnist for the* Los Angeles Times. *In the following viewpoint, written at the time of the 2008 presidential campaign, Goldberg argues that African American Barack Obama's campaign for president has not transcended race. Instead he says that Obama's supporters have made race central to the campaign by accusing all those who criticize Obama of racism. Goldberg argues that Obama has always embraced his racial identity, and Obama's calls for racial transcendence are merely a way to silence his opponents.*

As you read, consider the following questions:

1. According to Goldberg, what words or phrases when linked to Obama have been decried as racist?

2. Why was J. Edgar Hoover not racist when he referred to W.E.B. Du Bois as a "socialist," according to Goldberg?

3. What does Goldberg say is the overarching theme of Obama's memoir *Dreams from My Father*?

Transcend means "to move beyond, to surpass." At least that's what I always thought. But I'm beginning to wonder whether it means instead: "Much, much more of the same, only this time really stupid."

Race Dementia

Exhibit A: the incessant, relentless, click-your-ruby-red-slippers-and-say-it-until-it-comes-true mantra that Barack Obama [the 2008 Democratic presidential candidate] will magically cause America to "transcend race." One hears and reads this everywhere, but less as an argument than as a prayer, an expression of faith, a "from my lips to The One's ear" sort of thing.

It is, of course, total and complete nonsense. According to L.B.O. (Logic Before Obama), transcending race would involve making race less of an issue. Passengers on Spaceship Obama would see race shrink and then vanish in the rearview mirror.

Instead, Obama has set off a case of full-blown race dementia among precisely the crowd that swears Obama is leading us out of the racial wilderness. Rather than shrink, the tumor of racial paranoia is metastasizing, pressing down on the medulla oblongata or whatever part of the brain that, when poked, causes one to hallucinate, conjure false memories and write astoundingly insipid things. For instance, a writer for *Slate* sees racism when anyone notes that Barack Obama is— wait for it—skinny. What this portends for [cartoon character] Fat Albert is above my pay grade.

We need to rewrite those old Schoolhouse Rock cartoons, because now virtually any adjective, noun, verb, or adverb aimed at Barack Obama that is not obsequiously sycophantic or wantonly worshipful runs the risk of being decried as racist. Community organizer? Racist! Mentioning his middle name? [Obama's middle name is Hussein.] Racist! Arrogant? Racist! Palling around with a (white) terrorist? Racist! Celebrity? Racist! Cosmopolitan? Racist! This? Racist! That? Racist! The other thing? Oh man, that's really racist.

The new Schoolhouse Rock cartoon: "Conjunction: a word that connects a racist attack and Barack Obama."

This week [in October 2008], an editorial writer for the *Kansas City Star* denounced John McCain and Sarah Palin [the Republican presidential and vice presidential candidates] for suggesting that Obama is a socialist because he wants to "spread the wealth around." Don't they understand that "socialist" has always been a racist code word used by bigots like [former FBI chief] J. Edgar Hoover to demonize black activists like W.E.B. Du Bois?

A couple problems: First, as best I can remember, [Karl] Marx, [Friedrich] Engels, [Vladimir] Lenin, George Bernard Shaw, Eugene V. Debs, Norman Thomas, and Michael Harrington [all white socialists] do not usually get a lot of attention during Black History Month. Second, as writer Michael Moynihan recently noted, Du Bois wasn't merely a socialist, he was a Stalinist! (Du Bois was not entirely unsympathetic to the Nazis, either.) Besides, when did "socialist" stop being an anti-Semitic code word for Jew? Maybe when the Left started going batty over "neocons" [conservatives who support free markets, a strong aggressive military, and often social conservatism]. But that's a story for another day.

Obama Was Never About Transcending Race

The idea that Obama was ever really about transcending race flies completely in the face of his own writings. The overarching theme of his book *Dreams from My Father* [a memoir] is the story of a man who found it impossible to transcend race and instead explicitly chose to have a racial identity when he didn't have to (he describes fellow multiracial students he met in college as sellouts). He then joined a black church whose theology is shot-through with black nationalism and whose longtime pastor [Jeremiah Wright] believes that black brains are different from white brains.

But, yes, I know: The above paragraph reads: "Blah, blah, blah . . . racist racism racey-race-racism."

Now, let us actually transcend race for a moment. Apparently for Obama, "transcend" isn't a racial term so much as a euphemism for declaring victory. He says he wants to "turn the page" on the arguments of the '80s and '90s, by which he means conservatives should stop clinging to their guns and antiquated Sky God and join his cause.[1]

He told Planned Parenthood [a pro-choice organization] he wants to stop "arguing about the same ole stuff," by which he means he wants people who disagree with his absolute support for government-funded abortion on demand to shut up already.

He doesn't want to argue about his pals from the Weather Underground[2] who murdered or celebrated the murder of policemen and other Americans, he just wants everyone to agree no one should care.

In short, Obama and his disciples only demand one kind of transcendence from all Americans. We must, as Obama likes to say, unite as one people, one nation, one American family and transcend all of our misgivings about Barack Obama. Then, and only then, will The One fulfill his wife's pledge and fix our broken souls.

Only a racist could possibly disagree.

---

1. In the 2008 campaign, Obama said that people in small-town Pennsylvania who were bitter about job losses would understandably "cling to guns or religion or antipathy toward people who aren't like them."
2. Obama had some contact with Bill Ayers, a founder of the Weather Underground Organization, a radical Communist group that bombed public buildings during the 1960s and 1970s.

> "Whether you describe it as the dawning of a post-racial age or just the end of white America, we're approaching a demographic tipping point."

Demographic Change Is Creating a Post-Racial Society

Hua Hsu

Hua Hsu teaches English at Vassar College and writes for the Atlantic. *In the following viewpoint, he argues that demographic change will make whites a minority sometime in the next decades. Hsu argues that this change has helped spark a pop-culture interest in and celebration of diversity. This, he says, has led to some backlash and racial resentment among whites. However, Hsu concludes, ultimately America seems to be moving toward a world where race becomes only one among many markers of identity.*

As you read, consider the following questions:

1. Why does Hsu say that interracial marriage may push the moment of minority-majority America further into the future?

2. Why has hip hop's acceptance by mainstream America differed from Elvis Presley's mainstreaming of rock and roll, according to Hsu?

3. How does Hsu say that advertising strategy has changed to reflect a focus on diversity?

Whether you describe it as the dawning of a post-racial age or just the end of white America, we're approaching a profound demographic tipping point. According to an August 2008 report by the U.S. Census Bureau, those groups currently categorized as racial minorities—blacks and Hispanics, East Asians and South Asians—will account for a majority of the U.S. population by the year 2042. Among Americans under the age of 18, this shift is projected to take place in 2023, which means that every child born in the United States from here on out will belong to the first post-white generation.

Assimilation Is No Longer Necessary

Obviously, steadily ascending rates of interracial marriage complicate this picture, pointing toward what Michael Lind has described as the "beiging" of America. And it's possible that "beige Americans" will self-identify as "white" in sufficient numbers to push the tipping point further into the future than the Census Bureau projects. But even if they do, whiteness will be a label adopted out of convenience and even indifference, rather than aspiration and necessity. For an earlier generation of minorities and immigrants, to be recognized as a "white American," whether you were an Italian or a Pole or a Hungarian, was to enter the mainstream of American life. . . . As Bill Imada, head of the IW Group, a prominent Asian American communications and marketing company, puts it: "I think in the 1920s, 1930s, and 1940s, [for] anyone who immigrated, the aspiration was to blend in and be as American as possible so that white America wouldn't be intimidated by them. They wanted to imitate white America as much as possible: learn English, go to church, go to the same schools."

Today, the picture is far more complex. To take the most obvious example, whiteness is no longer a precondition for entry into the highest levels of public office. . . .

As a purely demographic matter, then, . . . "white America" may cease to exist in 2040, 2050, or 2060, or later still. But where the culture is concerned, it's already all but finished. Instead of the long-standing model of assimilation toward a common center, the culture is being remade in the image of white America's multiethnic, multicolored heirs.

Sean Combs as Great Gatsby

[A] moment from the *The Great Gatsby*: as [author F. Scott] Fitzgerald's narrator and Gatsby drive across the Queensboro Bridge into Manhattan, a car passes them, and Nick Carraway notices that it is a limousine "driven by a white chauffeur, in which sat three modish negroes, two bucks and a girl." The novelty of this topsy-turvy arrangement inspires Carraway to laugh aloud and think to himself, "Anything can happen now that we've slid over this bridge, anything at all . . ."

For a contemporary embodiment of the upheaval that this scene portended, consider Sean Combs [also known as P. Diddy], a hip-hop mogul and one of the most famous African Americans on the planet. Combs grew up during hip hop's late-1970s rise, and he belongs to the first generation that could safely make a living working in the industry—as a plucky young promoter and record-label intern in the late 1980s and early 1990s, and as a fashion designer, artist, and music executive worth hundreds of millions of dollars a brief decade later.

In the late 1990s, Combs made a fascinating gesture toward New York's high society. He announced his arrival into the circles of the rich and powerful not by crashing their parties, but by inviting them into his own spectacularly over-the-top world. Combs began to stage elaborate annual parties in the Hamptons, not far from where Fitzgerald's novel takes place. These "white parties"—attendees are required to wear white—quickly became legendary for their opulence (in 2004, Combs showcased a 1776 copy of the Declaration of Independence) as well as for the cultures-colliding quality of Hamptons elites paying their respects to someone so comfortably nouveau riche. Prospective business partners angled to get close to him and praised him as a guru of the lucrative "urban" market, while grateful partygoers hailed him as a modern-day Gatsby.

"Have I read *The Great Gatsby*?" Combs said to a London newspaper in 2001. "I am the Great Gatsby."

Yet whereas Gatsby felt pressure to hide his status as an arriviste, Combs celebrated his position as an outsider-insider—someone who appropriates elements of the culture he seeks to join without attempting to assimilate outright. In a sense, Combs was imitating the old WASP [White Anglo-Saxon Protestant] establishment; in another sense, he was subtly provoking it, by over-enunciating its formality and never letting his guests forget that there was something slightly off about his presence. There's a silent power to throwing parties where the best-dressed man in the room is also the one whose public profile once consisted primarily of dancing in the background of Biggie Smalls videos. ("No one would ever expect a young black man to be coming to a party with the Declaration of Independence, but I got it, and it's coming with me," Combs joked at his 2004 party, as he made the rounds with the document, promising not to spill champagne on it.)

Diversity and Hip Hop

In this regard, Combs is both a product and a hero of the new cultural mainstream, which prizes diversity above all else, and whose ultimate goal is some vague notion of racial transcendence, rather than subversion or assimilation. Although Combs's vision is far from representative—not many hip-hop stars vacation in Saint-Tropez with a parasol-toting manservant shading their every step—his industry lies at the heart of this new mainstream. Over the past 30 years, few changes in American culture have been as significant as the rise of hip hop. The genre has radically reshaped the way we listen to and consume music, first by opposing the pop mainstream and then by becoming it. From its constant sampling of past styles and eras—old records, fashions, slang, anything—to its mythologization of the self-made black antihero, hip hop is more than a musical genre: It's a philosophy, a political statement, a way of approaching and remaking culture. It's a lingua franca [something resembling a common language] not just among kids in America, but also among young people worldwide. And its economic impact extends beyond the music industry, to fashion, advertising, and film. (Consider the producer Russell Simmons—the ur-Combs and a music, fashion, and television mogul—or the rapper 50 Cent, who has parlayed his rags-to-riches story line into extracurricular successes that include a clothing line; book, video game, and film deals; and a startlingly lucrative partnership with the makers of Vitamin Water.)

But hip hop's deepest impact is symbolic. During popular music's rise in the 20th century, white artists and producers consistently "mainstreamed" African American innovations. Hip hop's ascension has been different. [Popular white rapper] Eminem notwithstanding, hip hop never suffered through anything like an Elvis Presley moment, in which a white artist made a musical form safe for white America. This is no dig at Elvis—the constrictive racial logic of the 1950s demanded the erasure of rock and roll's black roots, and if it hadn't been him, it would have been someone else. But hip hop—the sound of the post-civil-rights, post-soul generation—found a global audience on its own terms. . . .

Pop culture today rallies around an ethic of multicultural inclusion that seems to value every identity—except whiteness. "It's become harder for the blond-haired, blue-eyed commercial actor," remarks Rochelle Newman-Carrasco, of the Hispanic marketing firm Enlace. "You read casting notices, and they like to cast people with brown hair because they could be Hispanic. The language of casting notices is pretty shocking because it's so specific: 'Brown hair, brown eyes, could look Hispanic.' Or, as one notice put it: 'Ethnically ambiguous.'"

"I think white people feel like they're under siege right now—like it's not okay to be white right now, especially if you're a white male," laughs Bill Imada, of the IW Group. Imada and Newman-Carrasco are part of a movement within advertising, marketing, and communications firms to reimagine the profile of the typical American consumer. (Tellingly, every person I spoke with from these industries knew the Census Bureau's projections by heart.)

Is White America Losing Control?

"There's a lot of fear and a lot of resentment," Newman-Carrasco observes, describing the flak she caught after writing an article for a trade publication on the need for more diverse hiring practices. "I got a response from a friend—he's, like, a 60-something white male, and he's been involved with multicultural recruiting," she recalls. "And he said, 'I really feel like the hunted. It's a hard time to be a white man in America right now, because I feel like I'm being lumped in with all white males in America, and I've tried to do stuff, but it's a tough time.'"

"I always tell the white men in the room, 'We need you,'" Imada says. "We cannot talk about diversity and inclusion and engagement without you at the table. It's okay to be white!

"But people are stressed out about it. 'We used to be in control! We're losing control!'"

Children Under Five from Minority Groups, by State

In 2007 New York became the 12th state where the majority of children under five years old are from minority groups.

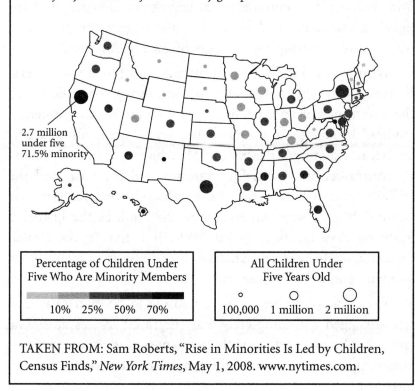

2.7 million
under five
71.5% minority

Percentage of Children Under Five Who Are Minority Members			
10%	25%	50%	70%

All Children Under Five Years Old		
100,000	1 million	2 million

TAKEN FROM: Sam Roberts, "Rise in Minorities Is Led by Children, Census Finds," *New York Times*, May 1, 2008. www.nytimes.com.

If they're right—if white America is indeed "losing control," and if the future will belong to people who can successfully navigate a post-racial, multicultural landscape—then it's no surprise that many white Americans are eager to divest themselves of their whiteness entirely.

For some, this renunciation can take a radical form. In 1994, a young graffiti artist and activist named William "Upski" Wimsatt, the son of a university professor, published *Bomb the Suburbs*, the spiritual heir to Norman Mailer's celebratory 1957 essay, "The White Negro." Wimsatt was deeply committed to hip hop's transformative powers, going so far as to embrace the status of the lowly "wigger," a pejorative term popularized in the early 1990s to describe white kids who steep themselves in black culture. Wimsatt viewed the wigger's immersion in two cultures as an engine for change. "If channeled in the right way," he wrote, "the wigger can go a long way toward repairing the sickness of race in America."

Wimsatt's painfully earnest attempts to put his own relationship with whiteness under the microscope coincided with the emergence of an academic discipline known as "whiteness studies." In colleges and universities across the country, scholars began examining the history of "whiteness" and unpacking its contradictions. Why, for example, had the Irish and the Italians fallen beyond the pale at different moments in our history? Were Jewish Americans *white*? And, as the historian Matthew Frye Jacobson asked, "Why is it that in the United States, a white woman can have black children but a black woman cannot have white children?" . . .

This view of whiteness as something to be interrogated, if not shrugged off completely, has migrated to less academic spheres. The perspective of the whiteness-studies academics is commonplace now, even if the language used to express it is different.

"I get it: As a straight white male, I'm the worst thing on Earth," Christian Lander says. Lander is a Canadian-born, Los Angeles-based satirist who in January 2008 started a blog called *Stuff White People Like* (stuffwhitepeoplelike.com), which pokes fun at the manners and mores of a specific species of young, hip, upwardly mobile whites. (He has written more than 100 entries about whites' passion for things like bottled water, "the idea of soccer," and "being the only white person around.") At its best, Lander's site—which formed the basis for a recently published book of the same name—is a cunningly precise distillation of the identity crisis plaguing well-meaning, well-off white kids in a post-white world.

"Like, I'm aware of all the horrible crimes that my demographic has done in the world," Lander says. "And there's a bunch of white people who are desperate—*desperate*—to say, 'You know what? My skin's white, but I'm not one of the white people who's destroying the world.'" . . .

Lander's "white people" are products of a very specific historical moment, raised by well-meaning Baby Boomers to reject the old ideal of white American gentility and to embrace diversity and fluidity instead. ("It's strange that we are the kids of Baby Boomers, right? How the hell do you rebel against that? Like, your parents will march against the World Trade Organization next to you. They'll have bigger white dreadlocks than you. What do you do?") But his lighthearted anthropology suggests that the multicultural harmony they were raised to worship has bred a kind of self-denial. . . .

White Minority Identity

The "flight from whiteness" of urban, college-educated, liberal whites isn't the only attempt to answer [the question of whiteness]. You can flee *into* whiteness as well. This can mean pursuing the authenticity of an imagined past: Think of the deliberately white-bread world of Mormon America, where the '50s never ended, or the anachronistic WASP entitlement flaunted in books like last year's *A Privileged Life: Celebrating WASP Style*, a handsome coffee-table book compiled by Susanna Salk, depicting a world of seersucker blazers, whale pants, and deck shoes. (What the book celebrates is the "inability to be outdone," and the "self-confidence and security that comes with it," Salk tells me. "That's why I call it 'privilege.' It's this privilege of time, of heritage, of being in a place longer than anybody else.") But these enclaves of preserved-in-amber whiteness are likely to be less important to the American future than the construction of whiteness as a somewhat pissed-off minority culture.

This notion of a self-consciously white expression of minority empowerment will be familiar to anyone who has come across the comedian Larry the Cable Guy—he of "Farting Jingle Bells"—or witnessed the transformation of Detroit-born-and-bred Kid Rock from teenage rapper into "American Bad Ass" southern-style rocker. The 1990s may have been a decade when multiculturalism advanced dramatically—when American culture became "colorized," as the critic Jeff Chang put it—but it was also an era when a very different form of identity politics crystallized. Hip hop may have provided the decade's soundtrack, but the highest-selling artist of the '90s was [country singer] Garth Brooks. Michael Jordan and Tiger Woods may have been the faces of athletic superstardom, but it was NASCAR that emerged as professional sports' fastest-growing institution, with ratings second only to the NFL's.

As with the unexpected success of the apocalyptic Left Behind novels, or the Jeff Foxworthy—organized Blue Collar Comedy Tour, the rise of country music and auto racing took place well off the American elite's radar screen. (None of Christian Lander's white people would be caught dead at a NASCAR race.) These phenomena reflected a growing sense of cultural solidarity among lower-middle-class whites—a solidarity defined by a yearning for American "authenticity," a folksy realness that rejects the global, the urban, and the effete in favor of nostalgia for "the way things used to be."

Like other forms of identity politics, white solidarity comes complete with its own folk heroes, conspiracy theories (Barack Obama is a secret Muslim! The U.S. is going to merge with Canada and Mexico!), and laundry lists of injustices. The targets and scapegoats vary—from multiculturalism and affirmative action to a loss of moral values, from immigration to an economy that no longer guarantees the American worker a fair chance—and so do the political programs they inspire. . . . But the core grievance, in each case, has to do with cultural and socioeconomic dislocation—the sense that the system that used to guarantee the white working class some stability has gone off-kilter. . . .

The result is a racial pride that dares not speak its name, and that defines itself through cultural cues instead—a suspicion of intellectual elites and city dwellers, a preference for folksiness and plainness of speech (whether real or feigned), and the association of a working-class white minority with "the real America." (In the Scots-Irish belt that runs from Arkansas up through West Virginia, the most common ethnic label offered to census takers is "American.") Arguably, this white identity politics helped swing the 2000 and 2004 elections, serving as the powerful counterpunch to urban white liberals, and the McCain-Palin [John McCain and Sarah Palin, the 2008 Republican presidential and vice presidential candidates] campaign relied on it almost to the point of absurdity (as when a McCain surrogate dismissed Northern Virginia as somehow not part of "the real Virginia") as a bulwark against the threatening multiculturalism of Barack Obama. Their strategy failed, of course, but it's possible to imagine white identity politics growing more potent and more forthright in its racial identifications in the future, as "the real America" becomes an ever-smaller portion of, well, the real America, and as the soon-to-be white minority's sense of being besieged and disdained by a multicultural majority grows apace.

This vision of the aggrieved white man lost in a world that no longer values him was given its most vivid expression in the 1993 film *Falling Down*. Michael Douglas plays Bill Foster, a downsized defense worker with a buzz cut and a pocket protector who rampages through a Los Angeles overrun by greedy Korean shop owners and Hispanic gangsters, railing against the eclipse of the America he used to know. (The film came out just eight years before California became the nation's first majority-minority state.) *Falling Down* ends with a soulful police officer apprehending Foster on the Santa Monica Pier, at which point the middle-class vigilante asks, almost innocently: "*I'm* the bad guy?"

Deemphasizing Race

But this is a nightmare vision. Of course most of America's Bill Fosters aren't the bad guys. . . . There will be dislocations and resentments along the way, but the demographic shifts of the next 40 years are likely to reduce the power of racial hierarchies over everyone's lives, producing a culture that's more likely than any before to treat its inhabitants as individuals, rather than members of a caste or identity group.

Consider the world of advertising and marketing, industries that set out to mold our desires at a subconscious level. Advertising strategy once assumed a "general market"—"a code word for 'white people,'" jokes one ad executive—and smaller, mutually exclusive, satellite "ethnic markets." In recent years, though, advertisers have begun revising their assumptions and strategies in anticipation of profound demographic shifts. Instead of herding consumers toward a discrete center, the goal today is to create versatile images and campaigns that can be adapted to highly individualized tastes. (Think of the dancing silhouettes in Apple's iPod campaign, which emphasizes individuality and diversity without privileging—or even representing—any specific group.). . .

The logic of online social networking points in a similar direction. The New York University sociologist Dalton Conley has written of a "network nation," in which applications like Facebook and MySpace create "crosscutting social groups" and new, flexible identities that only vaguely overlap with racial identities. Perhaps this is where the future of identity after whiteness lies—in a dramatic departure from the racial logic that has defined American culture from the very beginning. What Conley . . . and others are describing isn't merely the displacement of whiteness from our cultural center; they're describing a social structure that treats race as just one of a seemingly infinite number of possible self-identifications.

> *"It is clear that while the US now has a person of colour as a president, socio-economic conditions didn't miraculously change overnight for communities of colour the moment Obama won the election. Obviously!"*

Despite Demographic Change, Race and Racism Remain Important

Thea Lim, Andrea Plaid, Fatemeh Fakhraie, Jessica Yee, and Arturo R. García

Thea Lim, Andrea Plaid, Fatemeh Fakhraie, Jessica Yee, and Arturo R. García are all correspondents for Racialicious, *a blog about race and popular culture. In the following viewpoint, they argue that changing demographics do not mean the end of racism or of white institutional power. Instead, they argue, sweeping statements about the end of white America serve mainly to increase racial fears. They suggest that the popularity of diversity in hip hop or marketing has more to do with cultural appropriation than with real shifts in power.*

As you read, consider the following questions:

1. What terms does Fakhraie say Hsu does not define, and why does she argue that this is problematic?

2. What examples does Plaid use to suggest that racism can continue, even if whites were to become a minority?

3. Who does Lim argue are the poorest people in America?

So this roundtable has been a long time coming. In mid-January [2009] the team started to take a look at Hua Hsu's *Atlantic Monthly* article "The End of White America?" And we had a lot of pissed off things to say. And yes it did take us more than a few weeks to corral all our righteous indignation together. But we hope you'll think it was worth the wait. . . .

On Alarmism

[From Hsu's article:]

> What happens once this is no longer the case—when the fears of Lothrop Stoddard [author and political scientist] and Tom Buchanan [character from *The Great Gatsby*] are realized, and white people actually become an American minority? . . . Today, the arrival of what Buchanan derided as "Third World America" is all but inevitable. What will the new mainstream of America look like, and what ideas or values might it rally around? What will it mean to be white after "whiteness" no longer defines the mainstream? Will anyone mourn the end of white America? Will anyone try to preserve it?

Thea [Lim]: Hsu argues that mainstream culture has turned against white people and the way he talks, it's as if the colored hordes of [rapper and businessman] P. Diddy [also known as Sean Combs] fans and ethnically ambiguous Latinas who're snapping up all the commercial parts have somehow sneakily gotten hold of "culture" and orchestrated this shift.

"First, we'll make fun of you for not being able to dance! Then, WE'LL EAT YOUR CHILDREN!!!"

Andrea [Plaid]: This alarmist angle covers what really bugs me about the piece—it offers no analysis of structures and execution of racism itself in the US. What Hsu ostensibly and sloppily attempts to get at is once whiteness—and those white people and PoCs [Persons of Color] who adhere to it—fall back, racism itself will disappear. Hsu says:

> There will be dislocations and resentments along the way, but the demographic shifts of the next 40 years are likely to reduce the power of racial hierarchies over everyone's lives, producing a culture that's more likely than any before to treat its inhabitants as individuals, rather than members of a caste or identity group.

And there is Hsu's "we gonna be post-racial, y'all—if we're not already" statement—which can also be another read on this article. . . .

On Fear

Fatemeh [Fakhraie]: Hsu's "The End of White America?" (cue scary music) essentially aims to hash out the following: "Hey, white people are freaked out that people of color are becoming the majority in the U.S. Why's that? Don't worry, guys. It's cool." But instead of just sticking to this outline, it feels like Hsu tries to condense several books on hip-hop culture, racial history of the U.S., market trends, and race theory into one article. Because all of these subjects need extensive background, he fails in his attempt to mash them together.

Hsu hints at a "white panic" caused by the racial demographic shift, but doesn't explore it, question it, or even attempt to assuage it (except for a few paragraphs in the last section). He quotes Bill Imada, who states that whites are worried about "losing control," which is the reason for all this "white panic" over shifting ethnic demography. But instead of analyzing this point ("What do they mean by 'losing control'? What do they think this means for them?"), it serves as a transition at the end of a section, and is quickly glossed over in a comparison of different "types" of whites (the seemingly conservative and liberal camps) that still doesn't tell us what white people are afraid of.

Fear can't be assuaged or overcome without an assessment of what it is you're afraid of, which Hsu hints at in the next section but never actually plainly states: "The coming white minority does not mean that the racial hierarchy of American culture will suddenly become inverted . . ." As if people of color will suddenly disenfranchise whites, confiscate their assets, and force them into slavery.

Arturo [R. García]: It's hard to read this article without laughing at first, and then getting angry. Hsu's piece, much like Diddy's white parties he talks about, is high in concept but crass in execution.

Ask me about "the end" of whiteness when I don't have to read "reassurances" in the *New York Post* that minorities are advancing on television because there are more black supporting characters. Ask me about it when Bruce Springsteen isn't playing the Super Bowl half-time show because white people are scared of Prince's guitar and Janet Jackson's cleavage.

On Hsu's Use of Language

Obviously, steadily ascending rates of interracial marriage complicate this picture, pointing toward what Michael Lind has described as the "beiging" of America. And it's possible that "beige Americans" will self-identify as "white" in sufficient numbers to push the tipping point further into the future than the Census Bureau projects. But even if they do, whiteness will be a label adopted out of convenience and even indifference, rather than aspiration and necessity.

Fatemeh: Hsu presents terms that he doesn't define, like "whiteness," "racial transcendence," and "beiging." He also makes several terms synonymous that aren't so:

... the dawning of a post-racial age or just the end of white America. . . .

and

... we can call this the triumph of multiculturalism, or post-racialism.

These conflations are even more problematic because of Hsu's undefined terms; it's up to the reader to guess what he means by terms such as "post-white" or "post-racial." Undefined terms like this are unclear and often alarmist; I can just imagine a reader trying to figure out what "post-white" means: "Does that mean there won't be any more white people?!"

Hsu not only presents the "white panic" without a full explanation of what it is, but often feeds it with alarmist rhetorical questions like, "Will anyone mourn the end of white America?" and sympathetic constructions of white people who can't get jobs in advertisements because all the advertisers want "beige" people.

Andrea: Yeah, the word "beiging" is wrong on at least 30 different levels. Here are 4: Inaccurate, creepy, twee-rude (nasty with pinkie in the air), and asinine.

Thea: Let me just say that as a mixed-race person of colour I OBJECT to the word "beiging." Pullease. I am not beige! More of an off-yellow, really.

This is a long-ass article, but Hsu never finds space to define some key and rather obvious terms. Like "white." Or "post-white." Or "multicultural."

Hsu talks about how white people feel "culturally bereft" and want to distance themselves from "whiteness." And that seems an accurate representation to me—the word "white" has become a bad word. In some circles if you point out that Gary is white, everyone will act like you called Gary's mom a ho.

But what drives me mad about that is that it was the white colonizers who came up with the term "white" in the first place, to distinguish themselves from everyone else as more pure and biologically superior. Says Dr Gregory Jay of the University of Wisconsin in his article *"Who Invented White People?"*:

> It was white people who invented the idea of race in the first place, and it is white people who have become obsessed and consumed by it.... [Whiteness] emerged as what we now call a 'pan-ethnic' cateogry; as a way of merging a variety of European ethnic populations into a single 'race,' especially so as to distinguish them from people with whom they had very particular legal and political relations—Africans, Asians, American Indians—that were not equal to their relations with one another as whites.

So it's hard to have sympathy for "white folks on the run" or white folks who get their backs up when you point out that they are white, when it was the forebearers of said white folks who set up racial categories in the first place.

Perhaps one of the most infuriating things about this article is Hsu's expectation that we will have pity for these white folks who no longer know how to define themselves in a demographically shifting America. Because in order to have pity we'd 1) have to agree that this demographic shift was equivalent to a power shift, which as far as I can tell it is not, first African American president notwithstanding, 2) have to feel bad that white folks are feeling the pinch of a segregation that they have benefitted from for 100s of years—the segregation they started, and the segregation that many white folks only begin to notice and fuss about when it is *perceived* to threaten their power and identity.

Not to be all puerile and get into who started it, but uh, they started it. And to loop back to 1), I don't really care if you're being segregated. When you do a) become a minority race and b) become politically marginalised as a minority race, then I'll come and talk to you.

And anyways. What really has changed? Sure, I know lots of angry young people of colour who do see the word "white" as a bad word and use it that way. But I don't think they're the ones who are green-lighting films, owning the companies that can make or break a recording artist (like Sony or Virgin), or making the final decision on H&M's Spring Collection.

Hip Hop and Losing Control

Andrea: I think Hsu uses hip hop as a played-out shorthand for (and two of its proprietors, Russell Simmons and P. Diddy, examples of) "authentic Negritude," which is the image of black folks struggling in the hard-scrabble, poverty-stricken, school-system-and-city-government-failed, inner-city streets. I'm not saying that this isn't *a* reality for some black folks (and other PoCs as well as some white people here and abroad) but it also became the mythic standard of what [it is to be] an African American in the late 20th century and into the 21st century—and a commodified mythic standard at that. Hsu, then, uses hip hop to insinuate, "See, *those* uncouth, can't-quite-assimilate-to-'our'-middle-class-mores Negroes are taking over! Hide your (white) women and innocent (white) children!"::horror-film scream::

Thea: The fact of the matter is that this is an article that is not simply afraid that white people will be a demographic minority, but that they'll lose control. To me, that's kind of a repugnant fear. Would a little more balanced distribution of power across race lines really be that bad?

Fatemeh: Hsu doesn't ever address why there is such "white panic" by [right-wing commentator Pat] Buchanan et al. It feels like this panic is really a fear that white people will have to be treated the way they have treated people of color for years. Is this what Hsu means by racial transcendence? Why doesn't anyone just say this? I feel like that's what is meant a lot of times, but wrapped up in the secret language and given the code "power."

Are some white folks afraid they'll be forced into the white slave trade? Maybe. But I think most people are afraid of "losing control," which really means losing advantages over others because of skin color, losing skin privilege when it comes to housing or loans or job openings. People will have to actively work and participate in a community rather than assuming one exists based on race.

Andrea: Even if white folks became a numerical minority, I don't think that'll cause racism, especially white-centered racism, itself to cease. Unless my memory is getting rusty, a group doesn't necessarily need sheer numbers to have a system that works favorably for them—just the silver tongue and the ammo. (Apartheid in South Africa, anyone?) So, "white America" supposedly fading away in numbers and in "culture/cultural relevance" (both demeaningly ridiculous assumptions) will not make us "post-racial" any more than PoCs shutting up about Teh Racizim that "we" seem to be "foisting" on the "innocent" white people, esp. in the Obama Age, as Thea rightly states.

Jessica [Yee]: I mean, what's with the "What does it mean to be American?" question every time white people feel like they are losing power in these perceived "race wars." It was even in the title paragraph of this damn piece! Isn't it really, "What does it mean to be colonized, over and over and over again?" I think that's how one might fit in a little more with the truth of it all.

Like many people, I hate the quintessential pictorial of what a perfect, [homogenized] America would look like if we all just forgot our histories and pretended like we're getting along in perfect racial symbiosis. Diversity/equity work 101 myth dispelled for ya: Hiring people from racialized communities DOES NOT always lead to the appropriate programs and policies for people of colour. So take a chill pill about Barack, okay? (but keep on hoping for that change!)

Back to what people were actually saying for this article:

Bill Imada [chairman of a communications group specializing in multicultural markets]:

White people feel like they're under siege now.

Christian Lander [author of the book and blog *Stuff White People Like*]:

As a white person, you're just desperate to find something else to grab onto.

Matt Wray [sociologist at Temple University]:

You're forced as a white person into a sense of ironic detachment. . . . We're going through a period where whites are really trying to figure out: Who are we?

I suppose I appreciate the frankness of the opinions shared, although I'd be remiss if I didn't in my unpolite, non-Western norm discourse state that besides having had it with the same old, same old defensiveness that happens when racialized communities start reclaiming and re-asserting themselves, I'm at a loss for seeing how these various forms of wanted cultural appropriation, guilt-tripping, and blame-shifting the issues are in any way beneficial for improving race relations here.

Hsu also seems to suggest that with our increasing numbers, "armies" are going to form and white people had better watch out. Umm, yeah it's kind of exciting that we're populating the country as people of colour, even in Canada aboriginal people are the fastest-growing population with 50% of us under the age of 25. But are we planning to mass organize and take over the country the same way you f---ed us over?

No. Because culturally speaking, we wouldn't be aboriginal anymore. Thanks.

On Institutional Power

Thea: The article is peppered with quotes and anecdotes that echo this vision of white men on the run, of white men (well, really white people, but Hsu focuses on the men) being ostracised for being "culturally bereft" and lacking in colour. But strangely enough, in a 9-page article on power and race in America, Hsu never once talks about the real marker of power in America: money. Who are the poorest people in America? According to Wikipedia:

The US Census declared that in 2007—12.5% of all people, including

—10.5% white people

—24.5% black people

—21.5% all Hispanic people of any race, lived in poverty.

Stats on Asians and Native Americans are missing, but at a glance it is clear that while the US now has a person of colour as a president, socioeconomic conditions didn't miraculously change overnight for communities of colour the moment Obama won the election. Obviously! . . .

It is almost ridiculous to me that Hsu buys into the idea that Americans (and North Americans as far as I can tell) embrace multiculturalism and diversity *in a real way* when so much of the basic stats that measure well-being and race—the real measures of power—show that he is wrong. Here's some more stats: rates of incarceration by race in the US; and a Canadian article that states that

Although [aboriginal people] comprised only 2% of the general adult population, they accounted for 17% of the prison population. They were younger on average than non-aboriginal inmates, had less education and were more likely to have been unemployed.

Hsu never defines "multicultural harmony." And because some of his examples that pronounce the dominance of non-white cultures include white kids growing dreadlocks and suburban white kids wanting to be black (i.e., wiggers), by the end of the article I started to think that maybe Hsu believes that things like the use of models of colour in American apparel ads and last year's popularity of the fashion keffiyeh [a traditional Arab headdress] are examples of diversity's strength in American mainstream culture. For crying out loud. That's not power sharing. That's cultural appropriation. To go back to the first thing I said, I don't think it's people of colour who've directed the cultural shift that's got us suddenly slobbering over everything "non-white." I think it's white folks who are into cultural appropriation (i.e., not anti-racism or equity) [who] have made this so.

The fact is that the popularity of Eastern religions, sushi, Sufism, faux-Chinese tattoos, [rapper] Kanye West, backpacking across Vietnam and [reggae star] Bob Marley has not coincided with the fair distribution of socioeconomic power across the globe, or across ethnic groups in America. So call me a cynic but to me the popularity of those things—which more often than not rise to prominence as sanitised and whitewashed versions of their original selves—is more of an insult than a sign of multicultural harmony.

On White People Being Culturally Bereft

Arturo [R. García]: Life at the *Atlantic* has to be tough—how does one write this stuff with their pinky so high in the air?

Hsu's sources and examples are undermined just as easily as his argument. Really, we're supposed to be surprised that the guy behind Stuff White People Like would attest to a sense of white self-loathing? Did Professor Wray not refer his culturally envious students to Temple's genealogy department? Did he not teach them the meaning of the word genealogy? I've got news for these guys—some of the white people I know cared enough to learn about how their families emigrated to this country from Scotland, or from Ireland, or from Germany, or from Russia.

Let me repeat: They cared enough to learn. Only a narcissist (or worse, an avaricious hipster preying on the insecurities of people in skinny jeans) would dismiss culture as nothing more than a pigment; a shared history, the traditions, the customs and courtesies and the stories we learn from our loved ones help forge our respective cultures, not because they're "cool and oppositional," but because they come from inside us.

Hsu's "Flight to Whiteness" section, which could have examined the paths and reasons behind the remaining vestiges of generational racism, instead seems to buy into the self-stylings of the Cable Guys and Sarah Palins [referring to comedian Larry the Cable Guy and 2008 vice presidential candidate Sarah Palin, respectively] of the world as a would-be rebellion against the Evil Multicultural Empire. Instead of focusing on *Smokey and the Bandit* [a 1970s movie] and *Falling Down* [a 1993 movie starring Michael Douglas], he might have been better served asking how and why Michael Steele [African American chairman of the Republican National Committee] and Bobby Jindal [the Indian American governor of Louisiana] could rise up the ranks of the Republican Party to which so many of these "besieged" white people pledge fealty.

Arturo: Instead of asking the questions he should've, Hsu blithely dismisses race as "a fiction that often does more harm than good" and hides behind advertising reps eager to re-code and re-demo the young people they're probably eager to pitch cigarettes and nose jobs to before closing his note with hopeful visions of the upcoming social shifts—the same ones he and his editors had been so alarmed about. The "end of white America"? I'll just be glad to see the end of articles like these.

Fatemeh: This article was too tangential and incredibly disappointing. Hsu didn't need to dance around the definition of whiteness. He didn't need to use "whiteness studies" to dissect whites into different cultural groups (this should have been an entirely different and separately interesting article). He didn't need to compare P. Diddy to the Great Gatsby. All he needed to do was examine the white panic, deconstruct it, and let the anxiety around it float away after a clear, rational repudiation. Instead, he tried to come at it from too many angles, which just ups white America's anxiety level and feeds the fires of fear.

Thea: This article is a bizarre and sprawling mess that suggests that just because [hip-hop businessman] Russell Simmons is massively successful, America has not only achieved racial harmony, but is now threatening to submerge white folks into a sea of "beigeness." But it never answers a very basic question: What do any of the things that Hsu mentions—like Smirnoff ads, 50 Cent, Dora the Explorer or Stuff White People Like—have to do with actual rates of racial equity?

Not much.

> "What is currently happening today, though, for at least some slices of the Latino and Asian populations, is assimilation in ways that mirror the experiences of the Irish and Italians."

Asians and Latinos May Come to Be Perceived as White

Charles A. Gallagher

Charles A. Gallagher is a professor of sociology, social work, and criminal justice at La Salle University in Philadelphia. In the following viewpoint, he argues that Italian and Irish immigrants were perceived as not white when they first arrived in the United States in the nineteenth and twentieth centuries. They eventually assimilated and became perceived as white. Gallagher suggests that a similar process is under way with light-skinned Latino and Asian immigrants. He is concerned, however, that the process in America whereby different ethnic groups gain white status and privilege may depend upon continued racism directed against blacks and those with darker skins.

Charles A. Gallagher, "In-Between Racial Status, Mobility and the Promise of Assimilation: Irish, Italians Yesterday, Latinos and Asians Today," *Multiracial Americans and Social Class: The Influence of Social Class on Racial Identity*, Copyright © 2010 by Routledge. Reproduced by permission of Taylor & Francis Books UK.

As you read, consider the following questions:

1. Who are Keanu Reeves, Tiger Woods, and Barack Obama, and how do they suggest the changing nature of racial identity, according to Gallagher?

2. Why does Gallagher say that the religion of Irish and Italians result in prejudice against them?

3. According to Gallagher, how do marriage patterns influence the assimilation of Asians and Latinos in the United States?

Nonwhite racial designations are not commonly used today to describe "white" European immigrants who came to America between 1845 and 1924. Generations of assimilation have "whitewashed" the in-between racial status they once occupied. We tend to think of these immigrants as white *and* ethnic whose children or grandchildren would eventually lose their ethnic heritage and blend seamlessly into the dominant group. If, however, one takes a more expansive view of race to include the intersection of ethnic identity, conflicting racial ideologies and how class standing was implicated in this process of group identification, we can see how these immigrants were not considered members of the white race when they landed in the United States but "became" members of the white race over subsequent generations. James Baldwin reflected on the WOA (white on arrival) process by noting among European immigrants "No one was white before he/she came to America. It took generations and a vast amount of coercion, before this became a white country."

Racial Assimilation

The empirical question that is currently the focus of much sociological attention is if certain parts of the Latino and Asian populations, because of their unique circumstances and the changing demographic profile of the United States, are forcing a recalibration of the existing racial order in much the same way that Italians and Irish changed how racial groups were defined. Are Latinos and Asians experiencing today the same process of assimilation, both the loss of ethnic identity and the absorption into the dominant racial group, that the Irish and Italians experienced one hundred years ago? Or is the contemporary situation more complicated, and if so why? What social forces are at work that make it possible for a group to move from being viewed as "racial in-betweens" or "apprentice Caucasians" upon arrival to the United States to being unambiguously defined as white in only a few generations? Finally, what parallels can we draw between the past experiences of Italian and Irish Americans and those of Latino and Asian Americans today? . . . What role does class location and socioeconomic mobility play in reconstituting racial boundaries? . . .

If the idea that Italians and Irish would be considered "off-white" or "apprentice Caucasians" seems incomprehensible, think about how some well-known celebrities who define themselves as multiracial today would have been labeled a century ago. Actor Keanu Reeves is one-quarter Chinese, one-quarter Hawai'ian and one-half English. Through much of U.S. history Reeves would have been defined by the U.S. Census as "Oriental." Golfing great Tiger Woods defines himself as Cablinasian or (Ca)ucasian, (bl)ack, (In)dian and Asian. In 1900 Woods would have been defined as "quadroon" or a "mulatto" or perhaps "Negro" (quadroon is a person that is one-fourth black). President Barack Obama's mother was a white woman from Kansas and his father was a black man from Kenya. One hundred years ago President Obama would have been defined as a "Negro" (or perhaps a mulatto). Today these individuals can claim their multiracial heritage as a legitimate, recognized in-between identity. The claim of multiracial would have been a difficult one to make one hundred or even fifty years ago. Historically, the "one drop" rule defined any individual with one drop of nonwhite blood as being a racial minority. . . .

What is important to note is that the idea of who was allowed into the category white and who should be excluded has changed over time. . . .

The social factor that had perhaps the most profound influence on complicating and reinforcing the color line in the United States was the massive immigration that took place during the nineteenth and twentieth centuries. . . .

The years between 1840 and 1924 book-end a period of phenomenal migration to the United States, including millions of immigrants from Ireland and Italy. After shutting the borders to almost all new immigrants in 1924, immigration law was relatively restricted for another forty years, until the Immigration and Nationality Act of 1965 made it possible once again for new waves of immigrants to enter the United States. The past several decades have seen another large infusion of immigrants into the United States. The majority of this new wave of newcomers, however, came from Mexico, Central America, and Asia rather than Europe.

The Irish and Italians

The Irish had been in the United States since the colonial period but their numbers swelled in the middle of the nineteenth century due to the potato famine in Ireland. . . . Both a devastating potato blight that destroyed a majority of the country's food supply and political, religious and economic oppression by the English pushed millions of Irish Catholics to the United States between 1850 and 1900.

Italians who emigrated to the United States in the latter part of the nineteenth century did not experience the same intensity of religious persecution as Irish Catholics did in their homeland, but, like the Irish, they were extremely poor landless peasant farmers who experienced the same types of crop failures that were quite literally starving the rural population. Like the Irish Catholics, southern Italians were a pariah group in their own country. Southern Italians, those residing south of Rome, were considered second-class citizens by the more affluent and cosmopolitan Italians who lived in the northern part of the country.

The Irish and Italian immigration experience overlaps in ways that are meaningful for our discussion of shifting racial identities because these groups at one time occupied an identity that could be seen as being an intermediate racial category that did not fit neatly into the preexisting categories in the racial hierarchy of the United States. Both groups were overwhelmingly poor farmers and laborers and came to the United States at a time when nativism and xenophobia were rampant. Both these groups were overwhelmingly Catholic, arriving in a Protestant country that was historically and actively hostile to Catholics. It is not an exaggeration to suggest that the Catholic emigrants who arrived in the United States in the nineteenth century were viewed with the same suspicion and contempt by the Protestant establishment that Muslim immigrants experience today.

When they first arrived in the United States, both the Irish and Italians were forced into a vicious circle where race-based stereotypes defined each group and those pejorative labels became the justification for discriminatory treatment. While there were distinctions between the two groups in the stereotypes, they were both deemed by the dominant white Protestant classes as lazy, criminal, anti-intellectual, uncivilized, and barbaric. Therefore, while culturally quite distinct from one another, Irish and Italian immigrants both faced upon arrival in the United States systemic discrimination, racialized ethnocentrism, and mistreatment at the hands of members of the "native" white Protestant establishment.

The alleged inferiority of Italians and Irish immigrants was supported by the ability of the dominant group to situate these groups economically and socially within the established racial hierarchy just above and, in some cases, next to black Americans. At the time, a pseudoscience had emerged that maintained the Irish and Italians were racially inferior to white natives. In a strikingly similar manner, Italians at the turn of the nineteenth century and the Irish of the mid to late eighteenth century were painted with the same racist, stereotypical brush as black Americans. The Irish were depicted as "low brow . . . brutish . . . simian . . . black tint of skin . . . constitutionally incapable of intelligent participation in the governance of the nation."

The End of Ethnicity

There is of course a crucial difference between Irish and Italian immigrants and black Americans. Irish and Italian immigrants may have been defined in relation to African Americans and subject to systematic discrimination and oppression, but in the span of several generations each of these European groups was able to shed the presumption of being a "lower" race and assert their whiteness. As these European immigrants assimilated, they in effect were "whitened." Being able to absorb themselves into the dominant racial group with tools most black Americans did not have access to (like the ballot box, equal education, and unions) provided them entry into occupations that allowed upward socioeconomic mobility.

Not surprisingly, the negative traits Italians and the Irish were alleged to possess were similar to the characteristics that the dominant group cast on to the Asian and Latino populations during the same time period. Prejudice became the basis for discriminatory treatment towards each of these groups, as well. Throughout the late 1800s, Asians were subjected to extremely violent acts, including beatings, lynchings, and the wholesale burning of Asian residential neighborhoods. Since the time large swaths of Mexico were taken over by the United States after the Mexican-American War, Latino Americans have been subjected to property confiscation, racial prejudice, and status as second-class citizens, resulting in generations of economic discrimination.

If we fast-forward to the twenty-first century and examine the socioeconomic profile of Italian and Irish Americans we find that both groups have experienced upward social class mobility. Despite the fact that the dominant white establishment used ethnocentrism in ways similar to racism to discriminate against these groups, in the span of three or four generations this population went from being labeled as socially undesirable newcomers relegated to doing society's dirty work to entering the ranks of mainstream white America. The "whitening" of these two groups could occur because they were able to shed their ethnic identities. It was the loss of their ethnicities, their assimilation to the mainstream culture, which allowed their whiteness to emerge as a central facet of their social identity.

The dominant white establishment used what we would now call ethnocentrism in ways similar to racism to discriminate against these groups. As their ethnic/"lower" race identity was lost to assimilation as they became more economically, politically, and socially integrated into U.S. society, the dominant group's ability to draw on and use race as the mechanism for discriminatory treatment was lost. This process of decoupling an ethnic identity from a racial one was accelerated by a number of events. From the 1880s until the end of World War I, white ethnics were forced to live together and share social space in America's cities. Conflict over jobs and housing was common and neighborhoods were ethnically segregated, but these animosities slowly gave way to accommodation. The result was interethnic mixing and marriage among white ethnic groups that had historically been adversaries. Among white ethnics in urban areas pluralistic communities increasingly became melting-pot neighborhoods.

The United States' entry into World War II created a deep sense of patriotism and nationalism that leveled ethnic differences while promoting a sense of being "American." After World War II, the GI Bill provided for the mass suburbanization of white ethnics and gave them access to higher education. Millions of whites of European ancestry were able to take advantage of low-interest government loans and move from their urban neighborhoods to brand new white suburban communities which functioned as America's new melting pot. This shift from city to suburb and the upward socioeconomic mobility that accompanied the move from the "old neighborhood" further weakened ethnic identity. By the time children and grandchildren were processed through the suburban public schools there was little left in the way of ethnicity for each of these groups. It would now be the case that those of Irish and Italian ancestry would automatically respond that they were white when asked their racial identity.

Asians and Latinos

The Asian and Latino stories of emigration to the United States are in many ways more harrowing than those of the Irish and Italians. All these groups were horribly mistreated but each successive wave of Asian groups (Chinese, Japanese, Korean . . .) to the United States and Latinos (Mexicans, Central Americans, Cubans) had to endure racism, discrimination and economic exploitation for multiple generations. The West Coast was particularly inhospitable to Latinos and Asians, pushing for legislation (the Greaser Act of 1855; the Chinese Exclusion Act of 1882) that denied them basic citizen rights and institutionalized racist practices against these groups. In comparison, the Irish and Italians were able to assimilate and join the ranks of the white ruling class in a relatively short amount of time.

What is currently happening today, though, for at least some slices of the Latino and Asian populations, is assimila-

Asian Americans and Assimilation

Most Asian Americans seem to accept that "white" is mainstream, average, and normal, and look to whites as their frame of reference for attaining higher social position. . . . Like most other immigrants to the U.S., many Asian immigrants tend to believe in the American Dream and measure their achievements materially. As a Chinese immigrant said to me in an interview, "I hope to accomplish nothing but three things: to own a home, to be my own boss, and to send my children to the Ivy League." Those with sufficient education, job skills and money manage to move into white middle-class suburban neighborhoods immediately upon arrival, while others work intensively to accumulate enough savings to move their families up and out of inner-city ethnic enclaves. Consequently, many children of Asian ancestry have lived their entire childhood in white communities, made friends with mostly white peers, and grown up speaking only English.

Min Zhou, "Are Asian Americans Becoming White?"
Chinese Scholars Association Website, 2007. www.csasc.org.

tion in ways that mirror the experiences of the Irish and Italians. No doubt there are real differences in each group's experiences interacting with the dominant group, the resources available to them upon arrival and structural obstacles facing them at their particular time of entry to the United States. Rather than point out the multiple points of departure concerning each group's trajectory in the United States I would like to list how they converge.

Like the Irish and Italian immigrant population before them, the racial label attached to Latinos changed over time.

They were once listed as a nationality, then a race, and then finally officially listed as an ethnic group whose members are asked to select a racial designation. In 2000, almost half of all Latinos in the United States defined their racial identity as white. In the 2010 decennial U.S. Census it is likely that half of the nearly 50 million Latinos who now reside in the United States will define themselves as white. A sizable part of this population will marry someone who is not Hispanic and most likely white. It is also the case that when groups defined as being part of a racial or ethnic minority marry out, they tend to marry someone who is white. Sociologist Herbert Gans points out that "about half of all Asian-Americans and light-skinned Hispanics now marry whites, and at that rate, they may be defined as near white in a few decades." Nearly 70 percent of young Japanese born in the United States marry individuals who are white. . . . When one parent is white in a mixed-race marriage there is a high probability that the parents will define their child as white. This is particularly the case if the father is white and the wife is a nonblack racial minority. To put these trends in their historical context, one must realize that until quite recently crossing the color line in marriage was to be subjected to arrest, violence, and public disdain. . . .

The Price of the Ticket

What then is the common denominator that links these culturally distinct racial and ethnic groups? What can we say about the experiences of the Irish, Italians, Asians, and Latinos that is not so broad and general that we are forced to talk in gross abstractions? These groups each had to negotiate color, class, and culture. As phenotypically white groups, the Irish and Italians were able to assimilate and gain acceptance into the dominant group through the loss of their ethnic identity and a full embrace of a racial viewpoint that was grounded in white supremacy. Researchers [Jonathan W.] Warren and [France Winddance] Twine suggest that an in-between status such as that once held by Irish and Italian Americans can shift to a fully white identity because, since "Blacks represent the 'other' against which Whiteness is constructed, the back door to Whiteness is open to non-Blacks. Slipping through the opening is, then a tactical matter for non-Blacks of conforming to White standards, of distancing themselves from Blackness and reproducing anti-Black ideas and sentiments." Moving from an in-between status to one that was unambiguously white required a price, and the price of the ticket was for these groups to accept and participate in institutional racism that defined American society at that time.

One indication that a similar trend is occurring among Asian and Latino Americans can be found by examining where groups settle. Asian and Latino residential communities in the United States are less residentially segregated than blacks. Douglas Massey found that even the *most* segregated Asian neighborhoods are in fact *less* segregated than the *most* integrated black neighborhoods. What this means is that Asian and Latinos will avoid settling in black neighborhoods if they can and when these groups settle in white neighborhoods the residents do not typically flee. In addition, Latinos and Asians share with whites a greater average level of hostility towards blacks than any other group. For increasing numbers of these groups, the movement away from blacks is accompanied by a movement toward racially identifying as white. Based on their review of how Latinos and Asians self-identify in the U.S. Census, [researchers Jennifer] Lee and [Frank] Bean point out that "Asians and Latinos may be next in line to be white, with multiracial Asian whites and Latino whites at the head of the queue."

Just as Irish and Italian immigrants were able to utilize their "white" appearance in their process of assimilating into the white race, Americans of Asian and Latino backgrounds with relatively light skin are most likely to move up the current racial hierarchy. A study conducted at Vanderbilt [University] found that shade of skin color has an effect on wages earned. Among Latinos and Asians "immigrant workers with darker skin color have a lower pay than their counterparts with lighter skin color." This was after taking into account the influence of language proficiency, education and work experience. What this research on "colorism" suggests is that, in the case of Latinos and Asians, those who start to mirror the cultural practices and physical appearance of the dominant group are rewarded for these actions in the labor market. The result is greater upward mobility compared to those who are darker skinned and less assimilated.

Latinos and Asians are an exceptionally diverse group culturally, but what is happening at the racial margins of each of these groups with high out-marriage rates with whites is rapid assimilation. It is now the case that light-skinned Latinos and later generation Asians, often in the company of a white partner, can move into a white neighborhood and not ruffle the racial status quo. It is also the case that within three generations most Latinos no longer speak any Spanish and are, from a cultural perspective, assimilated Americans.

Becoming White

Light-skinned, college-educated, assimilated Latinos and Asians will blur the white and nonwhite barriers as Italians and Irish did before them. Just as immigration occurs for both push and pull factors, this particular group of Asians and Latinos has been pulled and pushed into the white race. They have been pulled because their (light) color and socioeconomic status work to support, rather than threaten, the white-dominated racial hierarchy. The push towards whiteness is the reality that there are greater resources available to those who are members of the dominant group (high-wage occupations, quality public schools, safe neighborhoods).

Irish and Italian Americans came to be considered members of the white race as their assimilation provided them with the material resources that allowed them to move away from the menial labor that was seen as synonymous with being black. Occupational and class mobility along with the loss of ethnic identity allowed these groups to assert what they were; phenotypically white immigrants from Europe who had been denied the ability to claim that identity because of racialized ethnocentrism. Today, Asian and Latino Americans who are light-skinned and have high economic status, particularly those who have white partners, may also gain entry into the white race. Those who marry whites are almost assured that their offspring will be accepted as white.

The dilemma we face now is: If the color line is shifting in this way, what does it mean for dark-skinned Latinos and Asians? How rigid will the color line remain for those Latinos and Asians who do not possess the physical features, educational credentials, or class standing that allow part of these populations entry into the dominant group? And, if whitening is a crucial factor to entering the dominant groups and the material advantages this membership provides, what does this process mean for black Americans?

Periodical and Internet Sources Bibliography

The following articles have been selected to supplement the diverse views presented in this chapter.

Rejina Bartlett	"The Race to 'Post': Can We Handle Current Business First?," *Racialicious*, July 13, 2010. www.racialicious.com.
Patrick H. Caddell and Douglas E. Schoen	"Our Divisive President," *Wall Street Journal*, July 28, 2010. http://online.wsj.com.
A. Bruce Crawley	"Black Alabama Voters Wake Up and End a Post-Racial Political Career," *The Black Issue* (blog), June 21, 2010. http://theblackissue .blogspot.com.
Courtney E. Martin	"The Power of the 'Post-Racial' Narrative," *American Prospect*, February 2, 2010. www.prospect.org.
Nicolas Mendoza	"The Problem with the 'Hispanics Will Become White' Argument," Campus Progress, January 19, 2011. http://campusprogress.org.
Walter Rodgers	"A Year into Obama's Presidency, Is America Postracial?," *Christian Science Monitor*, January 5, 2010. www.csmonitor.com.
Noel Sheppard	"Cynthia Tucker: Voter Anger Is About Racism—'Fear of a White Minority,'" NewsBusters, September 5, 2010. www.newsbusters.org.
James Warren	"White Women Influencing Shift to Minority-Majority Nation," *New York Times*, March 12, 2010. www.nytimes.com.
Hope Yen	"Minority Births on Track to Outnumber White Births," AllBusiness.com, March 10, 2010. www.allbusiness.com.

For Further Discussion

Chapter 1

1. Would Nadra Kareem agree with Erica Chito Childs that many white people see interracial relationships as deviant? Explain your answer.

2. Would John Raible's concerns about interracial adoption be diminished if an adopting family lived in a thoroughly integrated neighborhood with many other mixed-race families? Would the concerns of Frank A. Jones be diminished? Explain your answers.

Chapter 2

1. Douglas S. Massey states that the rate of Mexican immigration is not increasing. Does that undercut Jason Richwine's arguments? Why or why not?

2. The author of the editorial in *The Sentinel* argues that the core of American identity is diversity. Does Souheil Ghannouchi seem to agree with that? Would you agree that the essence of America is diversity? Explain your answer.

Chapter 3

1. María Estela Brisk argues that some bilingual programs, especially those for low-status languages, may be poorly run and ineffective. Does Christine Rossell make a convincing case that all bilingual programs are ineffective, or only those she studied in Texas? Explain your answer.

Chapter 4

1. Jonah Goldberg says that Barack Obama "explicitly chose to have a racial identity when he didn't have to." Would

the writers at *Racialicious* agree with Goldberg that it is possible for an American to have no racial identity? Would Hua Hsu agree? Explain your answers.

2. According to Charles A. Gallagher, how does intermarriage affect the perception of the race of Asians and Latinos? Does Gallagher's argument undercut Hua Hsu's arguments? Explain your answer.

Organizations to Contact

The editors have compiled the following list of organizations concerned with the issues debated in this book. The descriptions are derived from materials provided by the organizations. All have publications or information available for interested readers. The list was compiled on the date of publication of the present volume; names; addresses, phone and fax numbers, and e-mail and Internet addresses may change. Be aware that many organizations take several weeks or longer to respond to inquiries, so allow as much time as possible.

American Civil Liberties Union (ACLU)
125 Broad Street, 18th Floor, New York, NY   10004-2400
(212) 549-2500
e-mail: aclu@aclu.org
website: www.aclu.org

The American Civil Liberties Union (ACLU) is a national organization that works to defend Americans' civil rights as guaranteed by the US Constitution. It provides legal defense, research, and education. The ACLU publishes and distributes policy statements, pamphlets, and reports such as *Deportation by Default: Mental Disability, Unfair Hearings, and Indefinite Detention in the US Immigration System* and *Deane & Polyak v. Conaway–Friend-of-the-Court Brief of the NAACP Legal Defense and Education Fund on the Relevance of Interracial Marriage to Same-Sex Marriage.*

American Immigration Lawyers Association (AILA)
Suite 300, 1331 G Street NW, Washington, DC   20005
(202) 507-7600 • fax: (202) 783-7853
e-mail: liaison@aila.org
website: www.aila.org

American Immigration Lawyers Association (AILA) is the national association of more than eleven thousand attorneys and law professors who practice and teach immigration law. Member attorneys represent those seeking residence in the United States on behalf of themselves or others. It also provides continuing legal education and professional services to its members and the public. Its website includes back issues of *Immigration Law Today*, commentary and summary of relevant court decisions, recent and pending legislation, and other resources.

Asian American Legal Defense and Education Fund (AALDEF)

99 Hudson Street, 12th Floor, New York, NY   10013
(212) 966-5932 • fax: (212) 966-4303
e-mail: info@aaldef.org
website: http://aaldef.org

The Asian American Legal Defense and Education Fund (AALDEF) is a national organization that protects and promotes the civil rights of Asian Americans through litigation, advocacy, education, and organizing. Its website includes annual reports, news stories, press releases, program overviews, and blogs focusing on Asian American issues.

Cato Institute

1000 Massachusetts Avenue NW
Washington, DC   20001-5403
(202) 842-0200 • fax: (202) 842-3490
e-mail: cato@cato.org
website: www.cato.org

The Cato Institute is a libertarian public policy research foundation dedicated to limiting the role of government and protecting individual liberties. It researches claims of discrimination, supports immigration, and opposes affirmative action. The institute publishes the quarterly magazine *Regulation*, the bimonthly *Cato Policy Report*, and numerous books. Its website includes numerous articles and op-eds.

Center for American Progress (CAP)

1333 H Street NW, 10th Floor, Washington, DC   20005
(202) 682-1611 • fax: (202) 682-1867
e-mail: progress@americanprogress.org
website: www.americanprogress.org

Founded in 2003, the Center for American Progress (CAP) is a progressive think tank that researches, formulates, and advocates for a bold, progressive public policy agenda. CAP supports affirmative action and immigration. The CAP website posts numerous websites and publications, including "Affirmative Action in the United States" and "The Right of Voluntary Marriage."

Center for Immigration Studies (CIS)

1522 K Street NW, Suite 820, Washington, DC   20005-1202
(202) 466-8185 • fax: (202) 466-8076
e-mail: center@cis.org
website: www.cis.org

The Center for Immigration Studies (CIS) is an independent, nonpartisan, nonprofit research organization. It provides immigration policy makers, the academic community, news media, and concerned citizens with information about the social, economic, environmental, security, and fiscal consequences of legal and illegal immigration into the United States. Its website includes op-eds, reports, publications, court testimony, and other resources.

Interracial Family Organization (IFO)

e-mail: team@interracialfamily.org
website: http://interracialfamily.org

The Interracial Family Organization (IFO) works to facilitate the cultural recognition of interracial/multicultural families and disassociate this culture from long-standing stigma by exposing and discrediting stereotypes. Its website includes blogs, essays, portraits of featured families, and other resources.

National Association of Black Social Workers, Inc. (NABSW)
2305 Martin Luther King Avenue SE, Washington, DC   20020
(202) 678-4570 • fax: (202) 678-4572
e-mail: harambee@nabsw.org
website: www.nabsw.org

The National Association of Black Social Workers, Inc. (NABSW), comprising people of African ancestry, is committed to enhancing the quality of life and empowering people of African ancestry through advocacy, human services delivery, and research. The organization is opposed to interracial adoption. Its website includes information about task forces, position papers, blogs, and more.

National Urban League
120 Wall Street, New York, NY   10005
(212) 558-5300 • fax: (212) 344-5332
website: www.nul.org

A community service agency, the National Urban League aims to eliminate institutional racism in the United States. It also provides services for minorities who experience discrimination in employment, housing, welfare, and other areas. Its website includes news reports and publications such as *Opportunity Journal*, *Urban Influence Magazine*, and others.

US Commission on Civil Rights (USCCR)
624 Ninth Street NW, Washington, DC   20425
(202) 376-7700
website: www.usccr.gov

A fact-finding body, the US Commission on Civil Rights (USCCR) reports directly to Congress and the president on the effectiveness of equal opportunity programs and laws. Its website includes press releases, information about recent investigations, and numerous reports.

Bibliography of Books

Geneive Abdo
Mecca and Main Street: Muslim Life in America After 9/11. New York: Oxford University Press, 2006.

Michelle Alexander
The New Jim Crow: Mass Incarceration in the Age of Colorblindness. New York: The New Press, 2010.

Terry H. Anderson
The Pursuit of Fairness: A History of Affirmative Action. New York: Oxford University Press, 2004.

Paul M. Barrett
American Islam: The Struggle for the Soul of a Religion. New York: Picador, 2007.

Erica Chito Childs
Navigating Interracial Borders: Black-White Couples and Their Social Worlds. New Brunswick, NJ: Rutgers University Press, 2005.

Aviva Chomsky
"They Take Our Jobs!" And 20 Other Myths About Immigration. Boston, MA: Beacon Press, 2007.

Terry Eastland
Ending Affirmative Action: The Case for Colorblind Justice. New York: Basic Books, 1997.

Karyn Langhorne Folan
Don't Bring Home a White Boy: And Other Notions That Keep Black Women from Dating Out. New York: Gallery Books, 2010.

Gwen Ifill   *The Breakthrough: Politics and Race in the Age of Obama.* New York: Doubleday, 2009.

Noel Ignatiev   *How the Irish Became White.* New York: Routledge, 1996.

Ira Katznelson   *When Affirmative Action Was White: An Untold History of Racial Inequality in Twentieth-Century America.* New York: W.W. Norton, 2005.

Randall Kennedy   *Interracial Intimacies: Sex, Marriage, Identity, and Adoption.* New York: Pantheon, 2003.

Stephen D. Krashen   *Condemned Without a Trial: Bogus Arguments Against Bilingual Education.* Portsmouth, NH: Heinemann, 1999.

Mark Krikorian   *The New Case Against Immigration: Both Legal and Illegal.* New York: Sentinel, 2008.

Heather Mac Donald, Victor Davis Hanson, and Steven Malanga   *The Immigration Solution: A Better Plan than Today's.* Chicago: Ivan R. Dee, 2007.

Douglas S. Massey, Jorge Durand, and Nolan J. Malone   *Beyond Smoke and Mirrors: Mexican Immigration in an Era of Economic Integration.* New York: Russell Sage Foundation, 2002.

Gregory S. Parks and Matthew W. Hughey   *The Obamas and a (Post) Racial America?* New York: Oxford University Press, 2011.

Soong-Chan Rah — *Many Colors: Cultural Intelligence for a Changing Church.* Chicago: Moody Publishers, 2010.

Jason L. Riley — *Let Them In: The Case for Open Borders.* New York: Gotham Books, 2008.

Rosemary C. Salomone — *True American: Language, Identity, and the Education of Immigrant Children.* Cambridge, MA: Harvard University Press, 2010.

Gail Steinberg and Beth Hall — *Inside Transracial Adoption.* Indianapolis, IN: Perspectives Press, 2000.

Michael Tesler and David O. Sears — *Obama's Race: The 2008 Election and the Dream of a Post-Racial America.* Chicago: University of Chicago Press, 2010.

Jane Jeong Trenka, Julia Chinyere Oparah, and Sun Yung Shin, eds. — *Outsiders Within: Writing on Transracial Adoption.* Cambridge, MA: South End Press, 2006.

Tim J. Wise — *Colorblind: The Rise of Post-Racial Politics and the Retreat from Racial Equality.* San Francisco, CA: City Lights Books, 2010.

George Yancey — *Neither Jew nor Gentile: Exploring Issues of Racial Diversity on Protestant College Campuses.* New York: Oxford University Press, 2010.

George Yancey   *Who Is White? Latinos, Asians, and the New Black/Nonblack Divide.* Boulder, CO: Lynne Rienner, 2003.

Index